SMALL STEPS
INTO THE KINGDOM

FATHER SPYRIDON BAILEY

SMALL STEPS
INTO THE KINGDOM

FATHER SPYRIDON BAILEY

FaR

To Veronica

Published in 2016 by FeedARead.com Publishing.

Financed by The Arts Council of Great Britain

Copyright © Father Spyridon Bailey

A CIP catalogue record for this title is available from the British Library.

Contents

Introduction

As an Anglican minister who was becoming Orthodox I assumed my training and education had given me a good understanding of the Church and its faith. Fourteen years later and now serving as an Orthodox priest I understand how much I had to learn and how much there is still left for me to learn. One of the realities for converts to Orthodoxy is that the depth of tradition, faith and practice is inexhaustible: conversion means entering a life of never-ending discovery. This is the case for cradle-Orthodox too, but very often converts have the added task of discarding the false ideas previously acquired in order that they are able to see the truth.

The purpose of this book is to share some of the things that I and others who have converted to Orthodoxy have learned and which would have been useful to have had laid out in a book like this as we travelled on our journey into the Church. I feel I must state openly here in the introduction that the perspective of this book is that the Orthodox Church is the One true Church founded by Christ and that there is only One Church. If this is likely to offend you then this book is not for you. I have no intention of criticising other Christian groups but inevitably comparisons are made between Orthodox and heterodox belief and practice simply as part of the process of explanation: again there is no intention to offend but the fact is we convert for a reason! But this book is not written with the intention of convincing anyone of the truth of Orthodoxy either: conversion takes place in the heart regardless of how informed the mind may be.

The process of becoming Orthodox can take a long time, and this is important. Someone once said that it is easier to join some Christian denominations than it is to gain membership at the local golf club. For some this ease of entrance will be a good thing, it will be a sign of openness and welcome amongst those groups. But becoming Orthodox requires that both you and your priest be certain that it is right. We come to Orthodoxy with many expectations, but the Church has expectations of us too. Some of these are discussed later but it is important for us to recognise what a big step it is we are taking. If we move from a Methodist to an Anglican congregation, our relatives and friends are unlikely to raise an eyebrow. But if we tell our family that we are becoming Orthodox there will be all kinds of questions. Of course part of this will arise simply because few people in the West are very aware of what Orthodoxy is, but there is something more beyond this unfamiliarity. If we already belong to a Protestant or Roman Catholic community becoming Orthodox is a move on from what we have known before. It isn't simply stepping from one denomination to another, it is embracing the fullness of life in Christ, it means a wholesale change in our understanding of ourselves and the way we live our lives; it is entry into the Church. There are very real differences between the Orthodox and non-Orthodox understandings of salvation and the purpose of life. These differences find their expression in worship and theology and so both faith and practice will be considered here. There are some topics I have not included simply because I assume that parish priests preparing people for chrismation will cover them. It is my hope that this book will be an aid to that process and that those preparing to enter the Church and those who have recently become members will find here answers to many questions I and others have had answered on our journeys. But it is my hope too that readers who have been Orthodox for some time will find here clarification of Orthodox belief and practice that will be of help to them too.

But let us always remember that there are two kinds of truth. There are the truths that are made up of facts, whether they are scientific, historic or even facts about God and what He has done in history. This kind of truth can be understood, analysed and communicated without any personal commitment or relationship. This kind of truth is a means to encountering the more important truth; Christ Himself Who is the living truth. We can declare factual truths all day long but unless they draw us closer to Christ they have no ultimate value. Even the demons know the truth of facts: that Christ is God Who was incarnate, crucified and resurrected, and that He will come again to judge the living and the dead. But knowing these facts does not lead them to repent of their evil. Our calling as Christians is not to fill our heads with facts in order to impress others or win arguments; it is that we may strengthen our understanding of what God reveals to us in order to know Him more deeply. We must not allow ourselves to have the kind of belief that the demons have that does not change us or help us to become holy. Therefore it is my hope that this book will help you to understand a little more of Orthodoxy with that one goal, that through the truth of facts you may be filled with the living truth Who is Christ.

Finally, let us remember the parable of the pearl of great price and how Christ encourages us to sell everything to obtain that which is most precious. Having bought the field and become Orthodox, our task now is to dig.

Who Is The Church?

"He who does not believe according to the Traditions of the undivided, universal Church is an unbeliever."
~ Saint John of Damascus

We begin with the most basic of questions: who is the Church and how do I know if I belong to it? This is a crucial question that every Christian should ask and also be able to answer knowing that they do belong to Christ's Church. As an Anglican minister who loved the Church of England, its people and traditions, I knew I could not say with any certainty that I was part of the One Church established by Christ at Pentecost in the Apostles. This chapter will address the Orthodox understanding of what it means to belong to the Church, how we know the answers to these questions and also what should our attitude be to those Christians who are not Orthodox.

The first point to make is that there can only be one Church. Christ did not establish different bodies, but One Body, One Faith, One Baptism. The Church is the Body of Christ which, though often wounded, cannot be broken into separate parts. The Church is not a human institution like other worldly organisations, it does not belong to man, and man cannot do with it as he wills or change it to suit his own desires, or satisfy the fashions of his age.

When we look at the story of the Apostles we see that when Christ was resurrected they saw Him, they believed in the event, they proclaimed that He was God on earth, and yet they were not yet the Church. This is important because there are many western Christians who teach that to simply proclaim a personal faith in Christ is sufficient to make someone a part of the Church. In fact only when the Holy Spirit descended on the Apostles was the Church brought into existence. God created the Church by living within human beings in a new and profound way. And the Apostles received Him together, they did not become the Church as separate individuals, it was something done to them collectively. And I use this phrase "done to them" deliberately, because though God offers Himself to us and does not compromise our free will at any point, it is only by God acting in us that we become part of His Body. Once empowered by God they shared this gift with others who received it recognising that they were becoming part of that same Body created in the Apostles. Christ did not establish something called *Christianity*, He established the Church. This is the Orthodox belief in very general terms which few Christians of any kind would object to, so let us look more closely to see how some groups have abandoned the ancient Church's understanding and why this matters.

To call the Church the Body of Christ immediately leads us to mystical ideas which are beyond purely rational descriptions. Theologians have drawn on imagery to communicate their meaning, often using biblical ideas such as a house, or a vineyard, a shepherd and his flock, a head and body and a bride in union with Christ. Wherever the Church is found in the world each community is a part of the one whole. This unity is expressed through shared sacraments and a shared single faith. Its unity does not only exist in an invisible, mystical nature, but through the faith it professes and its visible sacramental life. If part of the Body separates itself from either of these two things it ceases to belong to the One Body. Therefore those Christian groups that exist outside of the shared communion of the Orthodox Church do not belong to it. Neither do those heretical groups who proclaim a different faith. The word *orthodox* means true or right faith and worship, it is not possible to mix false belief and practice with truth and what is right.

As an Anglican I was only too aware of the differences in beliefs between different Protestant groups and I knew there had to be an objective truth: otherwise there can be no truth at all. If the different Christian denominations believed different doctrines, I wondered if it were possible to discover which version of the Church's teachings was authentic (in that it was the original faith given to the Church through the Apostles). Once I discovered that the Church had had seven Ecumenical Councils (ecumenical in terms of universal, not in its modern sense of multi-faith) which had confirmed the truth believed by all Christians and that these councils were accepted at the time by all who belonged to the Church, it was for me a simple matter of identifying which confession had remained faithful to those councils. There are other matters relating to the authority of the Church's teachings which are discussed later, but adherence to the decisions made at the Seven Ecumenical Councils is fundamental.

The image of the Church as a Body is held in common by almost all Christians and yet the meaning of this is not always considered. A body must have a head, and the Church maintains that its Head is its founder, Christ. The rest of the Body is completely dependent on the Head, like a living organism which receives its power and purpose from the head. But despite agreeing on the Church being a Body, there are Christian groups who then declare someone other than Christ to be their head: for example Roman Catholicism has the Pope and the Church of England identifies the monarch as its head. This reality has consequences; if we then apply the image of the shepherd and his flock we could ask who is shepherding other communities if not Christ? Rome may believe the Pope is able to make infallible judgements but no such authority resides in a single bishop in God's Church. In fact these ideas about the Pope (called the Vicar of Christ in Roman Catholicism) correspond to neither scripture nor the universal consciousness or traditions of the Church. The very word *vicar* refers to one who is in place while another is absent: the Orthodox Church believes that Christ is present, even to the end of the ages. This reality finds its expression within the spiritual life of the Church as its members continually seek the guidance and protection of their Shepherd.

The Church's authority lies not in one bishop but in its collective faith. When Christ said He would establish His Church on the rock, it was not Peter himself but faith in Christ as the Son of the Living God which Peter had professed which would be the foundation. And it is this same faith and secure foundation on which the Church continues to stand and will always stand until the end of time.

There has been a fashion amongst Protestant groups to speak of revival. But the idea that Christ's Body must be revived is nonsensical, and perhaps even blasphemous. The Body of Christ is alive with His Spirit; no work that any man can perform can ever change this. This Body is made holy through Christ its Head but also through the presence of the Holy Spirit, and also the holiness of its mission and calling, and through the holiness of the faith it professes. However sinful individual members of that Body may be they cannot remove this sanctity because it is not dependent on us, but comes from God. Therefore, no matter how unworthy we may feel as part of the Church we must always remember that while God calls us to struggle and repent, it is participation in His holiness which sanctifies us and makes us worthy of His name.

Christ warns us that a branch cut off and separated from the vine can have no life in it. There are a number of ways that we can place ourselves outside the Body of Christ. If we continually sin and refuse to repent then we are wilfully rejecting God's call. This is not to say those who repeatedly fall are lost, only those who, each time they fall, have no intention of getting up and trying again. We all fall and fall again. But if we deliberately reject God's call to repent we have rejected Him.

Similarly if we reject the doctrines of the Church despite instruction, and knowingly choose heresy (teaching contrary to that of the Church) we cut ourselves off from the vine. No matter how minor the schismatic may claim a matter is or how inconsequential to them it may appear, if a person rejects the doctrines of Christ they have separated themselves from the source of Truth; Christ. The Church cannot allow false teaching to exist within it since it is entrusted with the responsibility of carrying God's revelation through the generations: this is why the Church has always treated wrong belief as an even more dangerous sin than wrong action and has protected itself from heretics by ejecting them from the Body if they refuse to repent.

In the words of the Creed we declare our faith in a Church that is *Catholic* and *Apostolic*. First we must clarify that *catholic* does not refer to Roman Catholic, but actually means universal or complete. This refers to the whole Church in all places, it is not limited to one race or national group, but all men in all time are called to be part of God's Church. It is also recognition that the Church has received the complete faith that lacks nothing and is in need of no additions. The second term, *apostolic* is important in a number of ways. First it is through this word we declare that the Church was established by Christ in the Apostles. The gift was given to specific men in a particular, historic moment in time. The Apostles then passed on to others what they had received who in turn preserved their teaching because it had come directly from Christ. But they also passed on the gift they had received at Pentecost, the Holy Spirit, the One Who had come to guide them and give them power. Therefore those who received the faith from the Apostles recognised that they must receive and preserve that which had been given so that it could be given to those who followed after them. To ensure that the teaching was not changed the Apostles appointed bishops to replace them and blessed them with God's grace to continue the work. Therefore the Church is *Apostolic* because it continues to maintain the life and teaching it received from the Apostles in all its fullness.

If a Christian group has appeared in the last few hundred years and claims to teach the truth of Christ we must ask how it is connected with Christ or the teaching received by the Apostles. The Orthodox Church has protected these teachings and guarded the traditions with great care but modern sects have no link with the Apostles and cannot demonstrate that their teachings are those protected and shared through the generations. Of course many groups will claim they have discovered some lost interpretation of scripture that had been lost since the earliest era of the Church but this creates many more problems which are examined later.

But the Orthodox Church is *Apostolic* in one more way. The Church believes that in Christ death has lost its power, and that those who have Christ's life within them here in this world will not taste death when they physically die. We believe that the Apostles live on with the Church in Heaven and continue to intercede for us. Therefore we proclaim that the Apostles are alive in the Church today because the Church's unity extends from earth to Heaven.

In order to claim their place within the One Church many Protestant groups argue something called the *branch theory*. This is an idea that maintains that despite their differences in faith, all Christians invisibly belong to the Church since they are new branches that have grown from the same trunk. However, since the trunk they claim to belong to, Roman Catholicism, was itself cut away from the Orthodox Church this is a difficult argument to make. Claiming to be branches of a tree that itself rejects them (even Roman Catholicism does not accept the theory) is a strange understanding of oneness and unity. The Orthodox Church has always maintained that real unity can only exist within a shared faith. While some Protestants will try to reduce what they consider the essentials of the faith to belief in the Holy Trinity and the death and Resurrection of Christ, in fact the Church has always rejected such a superficial version of its faith. Beyond these most basic of beliefs the Church insists on the reality of the saints in Heaven, on their involvement in the life of Christians still on earth and on the support they give through their prayers. The Church teaches that the bread and wine become the actual Body and Blood of Christ in the Eucharist, and so on. These are not peripheral ideas, but essential doctrines which cannot be cast aside because they do not sit comfortably with a group's teachings. Of course, we are free to believe whatever we like, but to do so and then claim to be part of Christ's Apostolic Church is misleading at best. At the Seventh Ecumenical Council it was recognised that all heresy is equally damaging, there are not some heresies that are worse than others since they all act to cut us off from Christ. To dismiss or reject any of the revealed doctrines of the Church is heretical.

This leads us to the question of whether there can be salvation outside the Orthodox Church. While we recognise that only the sacraments within the Church have God's grace and the power to strengthen and purify us, we must be careful not to limit God's love and mercy. However, this is not to suggest that anyone can ever live such a good life that they have no need of what God offers through the Church, only that none of us can ever make judgements about another individual's standing before God unless they choose to reject Him by embracing heresy or other forms of evil. Though we can say that God pours out His Spirit on all creation and that His love for all people is equal, we know that within the Church He provides specific help which is absolutely necessary for us in order to be able to live the way He wants. Knowing this we might ask why we would risk our eternal condition by living even for one more day outside His Church. However devout an individual may be we must never imagine that personal fervour gives a sect equality with the Church. While members of heterodox groups may benefit from reading the Bible and trying to put into practice the moral teachings of Christ they do not participate in the life of the Church since they reject the fullness of revealed truth. Members of the ecumenical movement will often speak of an invisible unity that somehow supersedes the visible unity of a shared faith and sacraments, while simultaneously rejecting the true invisible Church which is the host of saints in Heaven. While some of the sects share a number of the Church's doctrines, there are others which are very much opposed to its teaching, such as the Seventh Day Adventists who deny the life of the saints in Heaven through a belief they call *soul sleep*. Our modern sensibility encourages us to avoid identifying such differences and indeed many heterodox use the language of love and brotherly union to insist that such differences be overlooked in order to maintain an outward peace. But the history of the Church is full of saints who rejected false union in order to protect revealed truth. True union proceeds from a shared faith and shared sacraments through which the true union in Christ is found.

The members of the Church all have equal rights and responsibilities as its members, and though it does have two parts, the clergy and the laity, this does not mean that one group is in anyway more privileged or worthy than the other. All members of the Orthodox Church participate in the life of the same One Spirit and all therefore perform their role as parts of the same One Body. The clergy has been given a role in leading spiritually the laity and in the rites of ordination God gives certain grace for this task, but the whole Church shares in the proclamation and protection of the faith. As Saint Timothy tells us, the Church is *the pillar and ground of the Truth* (1Tim 3v15).

The bishops of the Orthodox Church are equal among themselves in the same way that the Apostles were. There has never been a belief that a bishop of one diocese should have the authority to direct or exercise control over a bishop in another. However, the relative importance of the city in which the bishop presides has granted an order of honour amongst bishops which in no way affects the authority of their clerical rank. A bishop is a bishop whether he serves in London, Jerusalem or New York and the claims of the Bishop of Rome to have authority over other bishops was one of the reasons the Roman Patriarchate was excluded from the Body.

It often comes as something of a surprise to Protestants to discover that this pattern of hierarchy existed within the Church even before the Canon of the New Testament had been agreed. That the Apostles were bishops and that it was the bishops who eventually decided which books would make up the second part of the Bible is something many Christian sects do not reveal to their members. The Apostles always pointed to this hierarchy as divinely instituted and those they chose to follow them were ordained in special rites where God's grace was imparted. Despite some sects' attempts to re-write history, we find countless examples of references to bishops and priests in the New Testament (for example in 1 Tim 5v19, Acts 14v23, Acts 15v6, Acts 20v28), this was the structure of the Church from the very beginning and is an immediate outward sign of how different most modern sects are to the Church of the first century.

Since the Apostles there has been an uninterrupted succession of bishops which the Orthodox maintain is one of the signs of being the true Church. It has been the habit from the very beginning of the Church's existence for local churches to keep records of the names of their bishops as evidence of this uninterrupted line to the Apostles. This serves as one form of evidence that what is proclaimed by that community comes from Christ; it is not someone's opinion or interpretation of dogma. In America today there are thousands of Christian sects each believing different versions of Christianity, and without an understanding of how the historic Church has protected itself from heresy, is it any wonder that so many well meaning people who genuinely seek Christ are taken in by these groups?

Unlike Roman Catholicism which sees its catholicity as being rooted in communion with the bishop of Rome, Orthodoxy teaches that it is the people themselves who are the guardians of Orthodoxy. While the laity accepts the authority of their priests and bishops in spiritual and pastoral matters, (Saint Paul instructs *obey your leaders and submit to them* Heb.13v17) the truth is proclaimed as a common action between clergy and laity. There have been councils of bishops which have met but whose decisions have been rejected by the wider Church and so have not been recognised as authoritative. A bishop's role is to safeguard that which has been given to him and to ensure that the truth remains intact. But the laity has a role in ensuring that any bishop who teaches contrary to that truth is to be removed if he does not repent.

The word used in Greek from which we get *church* is *ecclesia* which originally meant a gathering of people. Before democracy existed in Greece the ecclesia did not refer to all people but only those who had been called out by the herald to speak and voice their views. In the Septuagint we find a similar understanding of the word where it refers this time to those members of Israel who had been called out to be followers of Christ. In this way we can see that the early understanding of the Church was as the true Israel, the inheritor of all the promises made by God to His people in the Old Testament. The Orthodox Church does not teach that those Jews who have rejected Christ continue to be inheritors of any promises since the new Israel; the Church is established in the New Covenant in Christ. There are some Protestant groups who teach that despite their rejection of Christ the Jews continue to hold a privileged position in God's plan but this has never been the belief of the Church. In the New Testament we read that in Christ there is no distinction between Gentile and Jew: the only distinction is whether we faithfully belong to His Church.

The Church is in some small way a reflection of the union within God Himself, the Holy Trinity: the eternal love of God that unites the Three Holy Persons of God the Father, Son and Holy Spirit. We are instructed to love one another even as our Creator loves us, to be one even as God is One. And yet we fail to love so often because we are weak and sinful. But this in no way limits the power and truth of God's Church, in fact on the contrary, it demonstrates God's infinite power in that he takes such broken creatures and unites us to be the mystical Body of His Son. This is our calling and its immensity should be a source of joy but also fill us with awe and trembling.

Church Structure

"Do not think that you maintain the true Gospel of Christ, if you separate yourself from the flock of Christ."
~ Saint Cyprian

Many people come to Orthodoxy wondering about the relationship between the different national churches and to what extent this will affect them in their parish. This chapter will set out how the Church is organised and how the different parts of the Church relate to one another.

As we have seen the One Church was established at Pentecost. The Apostles who received the Holy Spirit became great evangelists for Christ and established churches throughout what today we call the Middle East. Saint Paul travelled west to Asia Minor, Greece and Rome and Saint Thomas to India. The early Church consisted of a number of dioceses but the most important fiver were Antioch, Jerusalem, Alexandria, Constantinople and Rome. In each of these dioceses the bishop was given authority over the running of Church life and no other bishop had authority in another's region. With time these dioceses became known as patriarchates. When Rome split with the other four patriarchates it really was one local church separating itself from the Body. The next chapter looks in detail at how this split came about but it is important to see its true nature. This was not a division into two halves, East and West, but one leaving the four. It is not surprising that western Christians would give such authority to Rome since it is the only see established by an Apostle in the West while the East has many that are directly traceable to Christ's Apostles as their first bishops.

The Church began using the word *Orthodox* to describe itself as early as the second century to distinguish itself from groups proclaiming heresy; known as *heterodox*. It was after Rome's departure that the word became a way of identifying the communion of the remaining local churches. To refer to the Orthodox Church as the *Eastern Church* is incorrect since the term implies a corresponding western church of equal standing but this is not the case since the Church is, was and always will be One.

After the Church had experienced periods of intense persecution Emperor Constantine made Christianity legal, and since it was now the state religion of the empire it is not surprising that the organisation of the Church began to take on aspects of the civil structures. An example of this is in the way diocesan bishops came under the authority of the bishops of major cities or metropolises, known as Metropolitans (they were subsequently granted titles such as Patriarch, Exarch and Archbishop).

The relative importance of the cities gave bishops an order of honour (though all bishops are truly bishops) but not an order of authority over one another. When Constantinople became the permanent residence of the Emperor (from the time of Theodosius) the bishop there became second in rank to the bishop of Rome. In our next chapter we will consider how this order of honour has been misrepresented in Roman Catholicism. The local churches today continue to recognise this order of honour, those being recognised by all other churches in canonical order are:

Constantinople
Alexandria
Antioch
Jerusalem
Moscow
Serbia
Romania
Bulgaria
Georgia
Cyprus
Greece
Poland
Albania
The Czech land and Slovakia.

We should note that in some churches such as Moscow they are listed in a slightly different order.

These churches are known as *autocephalous* which means they are self-governing. In practice this means they have the authority to elect their own primate and bishops and consecrate their own Holy Chrism. The word originates from Byzantine legal terminology and literally means self-headed. There are other churches which are called *autonomous* which means they have a limit to their authority and must be given Holy Chrism by what is called a mother church. Within this structure younger churches are given support and oversight by a more established church. Although most autocephalous churches are national churches and so have differences in language and culture, all Orthodox churches share in communion and doctrine and accept the canons of the Seven Ecumenical Councils.

There are now over three hundred million Orthodox Christians in the world and so over time some boundaries between churches have changed. With the increase in migration around the world some cities have Orthodox living there who belong to different jurisdictions because immigrants have often wanted to maintain their links with their national churches. Although this may be understandable because of its importance in people's sense of identity we must acknowledge that this is not something that is seen as a permanent situation. Ultimately negotiations will have to take place between churches to recognise a single jurisdiction in each locality, but it is likely that this will take a long time (perhaps generations). This is important for the good order of the Church's inner organisation, to satisfy canon law but also for the effective witness that the Church has in those places. In many parts of the United Kingdom migration has resulted in a breakdown of national association for some parishes where congregations consist of a mixture of migrants from different countries as well as native British people. This is often encouraged by the use of the English language in worship.

For people in rural areas there may only be one parish that is close enough to attend and so there is little choice about which church to attend. In larger cites however, people who have no previous links with a particular national church may wonder which one is right for them. This leads us to a sensitive area because it must be said that some Orthodox communities may be guilty of over-emphasising the ethnic nature of their congregation. There are even stories of some enquirers being viewed with suspicion. Attitudes that create any kind of ethnic exclusivity are sinful and anyone guilty of this must repent. I must say, however, that in the many congregations I have joined for worship I have never known such suspicion first-hand and I have never been greeted with anything but generosity and warmth. This has been the case both in the United Kingdom and in Greece and unless I have simply been very blessed to encounter unusually friendly people it suggests to me that such attitudes are in decline. It may be that as immigrants have settled and their children have become more culturally integrated than they themselves, old barriers are broken down. Of course this is all anecdotal and one bad experience may be enough to colour someone else's opinion completely. But before we jump to criticise others too quickly we should also understand something of their background. After winning national independence from four hundred years of rule by the Ottoman Turks, many people in Romania, Greece and Bulgaria celebrated their national identity as something precious and in need of protection. As an Englishman I do not share this pride about my own national heritage because I have never felt it to be under threat. As part of the new freedom these peoples had was the opportunity to practice their religion as full citizens and for some, Orthodoxy became an aspect of this national and ethnic identity. But let us be clear, the Church has declared that allegiance to national or ethnic tribalism within the Church as opposed to belonging to the diocese of that area is a heresy (called *phyletism* by the pan-Orthodox Council in Constantinople in 1872). The Church exists beyond any one nation or race and to confuse the two should be rejected by all Orthodox people.

Therefore, when seeking a local church a good first step is to find one that conducts its worship in your own language. Having experienced the beauty of worship in the Greek language on Mount Athos I can testify to its power but I also know that this could not meet my spiritual needs on a permanent basis: we must understand the words of the services because they express the depths of our spirit but also teach us the truth of Orthodoxy. A great choir or majestic sounding congregation may create an immediate sense of wonder or awe, but if we are to be truly nourished we must understand what is sung. If we have a family that we bring to Orthodoxy as part of our conversion, they may quickly feel alienated by services in a foreign language if they do not completely share our enthusiasm. If we hope that our children will continue to worship once they have left our care it is essential that they understand the worship in church.

It is worth noting that for many Greeks who have settled in the United Kingdom their children may feel as British as their friends and English is often their first language outside the home. With awareness of this Archbishop Gregorios of Great Britain and Thyateira at a conference of his clergy, instructed them to ensure a sermon was preached in English every Sunday. I must confess that my own poor language skills mean the people in my congregations are given no other option but to hear everything in English. One of the reasons the Church of Antioch has had such success in evangelising large numbers of people in America is because of its willingness to worship in English. Congregations feel more able to participate in the singing and no one is left feeling like an outsider because of national identity. We should note that widespread emigration has often led to groups abroad being called a diaspora. While this term is appropriate for national and ethnic groups far from home we must reject it in terms of Orthodoxy itself. The Church is spread through many means, deliberate mission, the seeking of asylum or economic migration, but the faith is at home among every people: the Church is universal, for all people.

Despite sharing a single faith there are differences in practice between the different jurisdictions and it is important for converts to find out what is done locally. For example some jurisdictions will require all seeking entry into the Church to be baptised whether they believe they have been baptised by a heterodox community or not, while others receive converts by chrismation alone (more will be said on this matter in the chapter about the sacraments). Most Orthodox communities recognise all Christian marriages as being real while there are some who will insist that a blessing takes place. I have never heard of this happening in practice and I suspect that such an expectation would imply uncomfortable and difficult consideration of what the couple's life together meant before: my wife and I were married in an Anglican service and I have no doubts about the reality of our marriage. There are some jurisdictions which will not provide a full funeral service for anyone who is cremated and there are also differences in attitudes towards the burial of people who have committed suicide. While these differences may not have much bearing on you now, they may prove to be more important at a later date and it is important to speak to the priest about where the jurisdiction stands on these things. Certainly they are more important than the relative quality of the church decoration or singing of the choir which may make an immediate impact on us.

A final piece of advice is to avoid making judgements about the priest. Many of us come to Orthodoxy having read good books about great spiritual athletes and it is easy to form romanticised expectations about what the clergy should be like. If we come to church with unrealistic ideas the devil may use them to disappoint us and convince us that things aren't good enough and that we should look elsewhere. We must remember that the demons will do everything in their power to prevent us from becoming part of Christ's Church and our own lack of discernment can be a dangerous pitfall. The grace of the priesthood is a real and wonderful blessing but it is given to men of flesh and blood. The devil will delight in telling us how unworthy the priest is: but rest assured, the priest is only too aware of his own unworthiness.

What Are The Different Bishops?

"Anyone who acts without the bishop, the priests and the deacons does not have a clean conscience."
~ Saint Ignatius of Antioch

Having considered the structure of the Church we should pause and reflect on the role of the bishops. Converts may feel a little confused by the array of titles that bishops have but the matter is more straightforward than it may seem. The difference in titles may also cause hesitancy when having to address or write to a bishop and so this short chapter will attempt to clarify a few details.

The most important point to remember is that as successors to the Apostles all bishops have equality in terms of their ordination, it is a sacramental equality: the differences lie in their roles in governing the Church. It is useful if we imagine the bishop representing two aspects of the Church, each to the other. To his diocese, the local church, he represents the wider communion, the Church. But equally to the Church at large he stands as representative of the people in his diocese. His primary role is to uphold the unity of the Church in the One Faith by defending Orthodox teaching and practice.

At his ordination the bishop receives gifts of the Holy Spirit in a particular way in order that Christ may act through him. Orthodoxy maintains that Christ is present with us always just as He promised He would be, and so the bishop does not represent an absent God, but God as the eternal Good Shepherd acts through the shepherding of His servant. Bishops wear a vestment called the *omophorion* which hangs down at the front and back to symbolise a lamb carried over a shepherd's shoulders and in the ancient Church it was usually made from sheepskin. The mitre of a bishop symbolises a crown and reminds us of his authority while the round icon that hangs on his chest is a reminder to him that Christ and the Theotokos must always be in his heart.

Though priests too receive a special grace through their ordination they only serve in their parishes in the authority of the bishop. The cloth which is unfolded on the altar for the Divine Liturgy, called the antimins, bears the signature of the bishop as a sign that the priest has permission to celebrate the Eucharist, but it is also a sign that what is done on the altar carries the authority of the bishop and the shared faith and doctrines of the Church. Saint Ignatius of Antioch said *he who acts without the bishop's knowledge is in the devil's service.* The Church has protected the integrity of its faith in this way, ensuring that what is taught and passed on through the generations corresponds to the faith passed from Apostle to bishop to bishop.

The Orthodox Church selects men to become bishops from the ranks of monks and this has something of a surprising origin. In the fifth century the Church began to lose large areas of land when sons and daughters of bishops inherited the property. By ensuring that the Church kept its land it inadvertently ensured that for generations to come holy men of great spiritual stature would be chosen to shepherd Christ's flock and as is so often the case, God blesses us through what outwardly appears to be a completely pragmatic decision.

The titles given to bishops reflect not just the importance of the cities in which they serve, as mentioned earlier, but also their administrative rank: let us consider them in turn.

Patriarch was a title first given to bishops in the three major sees of the Church: Rome, Alexandria and Antioch. It was not long after that the bishops of Constantinople and Jerusalem were additionally granted the title. As the Church grew it was considered appropriate to apply the title to bishops of other important regions. Today however, we may notice that the importance of a particular city or area has declined but the bishops there retain the title. Patriarchs are addressed as *His Beatitude* except the Ecumenical Patriarch who is addressed as *His All Holiness the Ecumenical Patriarch.*

Archbishops are senior bishops who normally govern a large ecclesiastical jurisdiction, often with the assistance of auxiliary bishops. Archbishops are normally addressed as *His Beatitude the Archbishop of...* except in Greece, Cyprus, Great Britain, America and Australia where they are addressed as *His Eminence.*

Auxiliary Bishops do not govern the diocese in which they serve but assist the ruling bishop and are under his authority. Auxiliary Bishops are addressed as *The Right Reverend* or if they are assigned to ancient dioceses that no longer function are called **Titular Bishops** and are addressed as *His Excellency.*

Orthodox clergy may be married but if a priest is celibate he may be honoured with the rank of archimandrite which is a monastic rank. Since around the sixth century all bishops have been selected from the rank of single or widowed priests and there has been a strong tradition of bishops coming from the monastic ranks. While a married priest will wear the familiar black hat archimandrites wear a veil that falls down the back of the hat onto the shoulders.

Although our bishops are loved and treated with great respect the Church does not teach that any bishop is infallible. The collegiate nature of the Church is expressed through councils where consensus is reached through the guidance of the Holy Spirit. This leads us to the question of the Pope of Rome and his claims to make infallible judgements about doctrine. Our next chapter will address why and how the Patriarchate of Rome left the Church.

How did Rome come to be separated from the Church?

"The rock on which Christ will build His Church means the faith of confession."

"Behold how Peter does all things by common consent, and decides nothing by his own power of authority."

~ Saint John Chrysostom

The Great Schism was not so much an event that took place in 1054 as a long process that eventually led to the Patriarchate of Rome leaving the Church. Although there were important theological issues involved, most notably the matter of the *filioque*, there were also cultural, political and economic factors that played a part. We will first look at the wider context before focussing on the issue of doctrine.

The eastern and western parts of the Empire had for some time been growing apart. Political unity had been strained because the two parts had been ruled by separate emperors from the third century onwards and when Constantine created a second capital in Constantinople the message was clear. The western side of the Empire suffered barbarian invasions which not only diverted political attention but also caused the Bishop of Rome to play more of a military role in the defence of the Christian Empire. The sense of division was driven further when the eastern section suffered invasion from the sixth and seventh centuries by Muslims.

But despite these pressures Rome had continued to look to the Byzantine world for its understanding of itself until Pope Stephen in 754 A.D. turned his allegiance to the Franks. The Franks recognised the strength of the united Empire and in order to control the western countries knew it would be necessary to divide western and eastern Christians. This came to fruition when Pope Leo III crowned Charlemagne as King of the Franks, and bestowed upon him the title Emperor. In effect this created a political schism within the Christian Empire which weakened both halves militarily.

A further part of the process was the issue of language. The Church had been able to spread its message so quickly in the first centuries of its existence because amongst the educated classes Greek and Latin were in common usage: having these two languages was very rare even by the fifth and sixth centuries. This meant that the exchange of ideas was immediately more difficult and misunderstandings were far more likely.

While Charlemagne was not recognised in the East he also refused to accept the decisions of the Seventh Ecumenical Council. He accused eastern Christians of heresy for failing to recognise the *filioque* and the sense of shared identity was becoming a distant memory. However, it should be noted that during this time the Christians of the West were becoming known as Franks while eastern Christians still referred to themselves and were known amongst the Muslims as Romans as they saw a continuation of the ancient Empire in their culture. Later when the popes were sending armies on crusades the eastern Christians saw what was happening as Frankish invasions. Indeed in 1204 A.D. when the Fourth Crusade took place Constantinople was itself attacked by Frankish soldiers: churches were burned, holy relics stolen (many of which are still in Rome today) and women and children were raped and killed: treatment of the Christians at the hands of the crusaders was said to be worse than that experienced when the Muslims had invaded. Eastern Christians saw this taking place with the blessing of the Pope and anyone who doubted the reality of the division of 1054 now had all doubts removed.

A further divide was in the approach to theology. Western Christians were becoming increasingly influenced by juridical ideas, particularly in terms of Roman law. While the East saw this as a growing legalism, they themselves identified theology as something coming from worship and spiritual experience. There was also a difference in understanding of role of the clergy: in the West there was a growing distinction between laity and clergy, mainly as a result of the decline in education amongst non-clerics. In the East education was still available to the laity and there was a strong tradition of the lay-theologian while in the West theology was becoming the preserve of the clergy who had adopted the role of interpreters of the faith for the illiterate masses (no pun intended).

In the face of barbarian invasion the popes had assumed a military role which had developed into direct rule over all the bishops of the West. Eastern bishops did not concern themselves with these matters until the popes began to see their rule as extending over the eastern dioceses as well. The eastern bishops understood matters of faith as being decided in councils, not by a single infallible bishop and the popes' claims were a further cause of division.

But more than anything else the divide between East and West was over the *filioque*. In the Nicene Creed we declare our faith in the Holy Spirit "Who proceeds from the Father". In the eighth century Spanish Christians were dealing with a resurgence of Arianism (a teaching that Christ is not truly God but is a created being, as taught by Jehovah's Witnesses today) and so as a safeguard against such teaching they changed the wording of the Creed. The Latin word *filioque* translates into English as *and the Son* and was inserted to proclaim that the Holy Spirit "proceeds from the Father and the Son". This altered version of the Creed quickly spread from Spain into France and on into Germany. Some writers have argued that

Charlemagne saw the filioque as an opportunity to sever ties further between the Christians of the East and West in order to rule more easily. It should be noted that despite Charlemagne's accusation of heresy towards those who refused the new form of the Creed, Pope Leo had the original, unchanged version displayed in St. Peter's and up until the eleventh century this was the form still recited in Rome.

We might ask why the inclusion of a single word or phrase could have had such a dramatic effect on the relations between the two parts of the Empire. Orthodox opposition to the change consisted of two main points: authority and the theology of the Holy Trinity. The eastern Christians maintained that only an Ecumenical Council has the authority to make these kinds of changes since the Creed is the possession of the whole Church; it is the declaration of the faith of the One Body. Therefore to unilaterally change the Creed was a sin that risked the truth of the faith but also struck against the unity of the Church.

The second objection concerns God Himself. The Nicene Creed proclaims that the Holy Spirit proceeds from the Father alone and not from the Son Who is begotten of the Father. It is these properties of "proceeding from the Father" and being "begotten of the Father" that distinguish the Persons of the Holy Trinity. As Saint Gregory the Theologian writes:

What is common to the Father, to the Son and to the Holy Spirit is the divinity or uncreated nature. What is common to the Son and to the Holy Spirit is to have their origin from the Father. The attribute proper to the Father is to be unbegotten, generation is proper to the Son and procession is proper to the Holy Spirit.

The Church recognises the limits to divinely revealed knowledge of God: He reveals to us that which is necessary for our salvation. The incomprehensible nature of the Holy Trinity can not be defined by words: the divine essence is unknowable to us and even to the angels. Human reason cannot fathom these mysteries but God chooses to reveal Himself through His uncreated energies to those hearts that are made capable of receiving them. To change or dismiss the revealed truth is to fall into heresy and untruth. The filioque declares a false trinity that is a construct of human fantasy and is not the self-revelation of God. There have been many trinities proclaimed through history, even by non-Christians such as Plato and Porphyrios, whose false ideas lead to the worship of idols not God.

Western thought has been heavily influenced on this issue by Augustine, Aquinas and Anselm who falsely argued that God can be known through speculative philosophy. Augustine claimed that the Platonists had a knowledge of the Holy Trinity and so concluded that such knowledge could be gained outside of God's self-revelation.

Much of the western error has been based on a false interpretation of words spoken by Christ as recorded in the fifteenth chapter of the Gospel of Saint John. Here Jesus talks of sending the Comforter. There is universal agreement amongst the Fathers that these words do not reveal the eternal relationship between the Second and Third Persons of the Holy Trinity but the historical sending, within time, of the Holy Spirit at Pentecost as part of the economy of our salvation.

The *filioque* distorts the relationships within the Holy Trinity. While attempting to defend the divinity of Christ by elevating Him in this way the effect is actually to demote the Holy Spirit. It is not unusual to read Roman writers speaking of the Holy Spirit as "it" because His true Personhood has been abandoned, reducing Him to an effect or manifestation of the love between the two Persons of the Father and Son. Certainly Thomas Aquinas taught that the Holy Spirit is the Divine Love rather than the Divine Hypostasis (Person). This has resulted in many common western prayers being concluded "in the unity of the Holy Spirit". In fact the Church maintains that the Uncreated Energy of Divine Love is common to all three Divine Persons. By reducing the Holy Spirit in this way the western heresy denies the reality of the Holy Trinity. This has led some theologians to question whether in fact the god of Rome is no more than an idolatrous construct.

The underlying issue in this heresy is really about the Three persons themselves. While the Church received the truth of the Three, specific Divine Persons, the filioque leads western thinkers to see the Holy Trinity as merely a manifestation of the relations within the divine essence. The filioque erodes the distinctiveness of the Father and the Son, and Aquinas rejects the truth of the Holy Trinity through this notion of relations within the essence. The problem is that these thinkers have begun with their own reasoning and philosophical fantasies rather than the revealed truth. Since the Church has direct experience of God it has no need of such false ideas.

The consequences of this heresy are most destructive in terms of the understanding of the Church. Since the Holy Spirit is no longer recognised as the full Third Person of the Holy Trinity, He is not recognised as bringing to man the deifying energy of God (see later notes on Theosis). The Church is not seen to have God Himself dwelling within it and so Rome has invented intermediaries such as the Pope to mediate between God and man. The western God is not truly Holy Trinity and so it is not surprising that so many western thinkers see no difficulty in identifying the God of Islam or various pagan groups with the God of Christianity. The ecumenical movement is founded on a false and idolatrous concept which is not God.

In 431 A.D. the Third Ecumenical Council ruled that nothing in the Creed can be changed. The consensus of the early Church was expressed through the guidance of the Holy Spirit. The Nicene Creed does not provide us with a buffet of beliefs from which we are free to select what takes our fancy. The Creed is prescriptive, it teaches the revealed truth and if we wish to belong to Christ's Church we must profess that one unchanged truth. Neither do we believe that the Creed derives its authority from the Bible, it is not dependent on what is recorded there, but is in itself a divine revelation. To allow the Pope to insert additional clauses into the Creed is to declare the Pope above both the Creed and the Ecumenical Councils. It gives the Pope an authority not just over all Christians of his day but over those in the past too.

In addition to this central doctrinal difference there were other practices and beliefs that contributed to the schism. In the eastern part of the Empire priests were permitted to marry while Latin practice insisted on their celibacy. There also developed different rules about fasting and while eastern Christians used leavened bread in the Eucharist the Latins introduced unleavened wafers: despite all this, relations between the two halves of the Empire had been maintained. But in 858 A.D. Photius the Great was appointed Patriarch of Constantinople and he came into dispute over the previous Patriarch Ignatius who had been exiled. Pope Nicolas saw it as an opportunity to flex his papal authority and tried to intervene in the matter and claimed to have authority "over all the earth, over every church". The dispute widened and eventually Photius called a council in 867 A.D. and declared Pope Nicolas to be excommunicated and identified him as a heretic. Further disputes arose but the single Empire was still outwardly maintained. But as the eleventh century began the filioque was included as the Creed was sung at the coronation of Emperor Henry in Rome. As a result the Pope was removed from the diptychs in Constantinople which set the path for what was to come.

Finally in 1054 there was a Norman attack on Byzantine communities in Italy who were forced under terrible threats to conform to Latin practices. The culmination of the political back and forth was that Pope Leo sent three legates to Constantinople. Problems were not resolved and one of the legates, Bishop Humbert of Silva Candida, placed a bull of excommunication on the altar of the Church of the Holy Wisdom.

This was the moment when the technical process of schism came into play but even after this event ordinary Christians continued as they had always done in terms of their dealings with one another across the East-West divide. It could be argued that it was the crusades which finally brought into focus the reality of schism for many people, especially when the Latins attempted to establish their own Patriarchs in Antioch and Jerusalem. But doctrinal issues sit at the heart of the schism. So long as western Christians use an altered version of the Creed moves to reconciliation cannot begin. The Church is not in error, and as with the heretics of the past, reconciliation can only happen when heresy is renounced and repentance leads people to turn back to Christ's Church. Protestants, too, must recognise their traditions as having grown from a schismatic organisation and ultimately question how their groups can claim to have any link with the historical Church of the Apostles.

The Sources Of Authority In The Church

"As we acknowledge One God, so too there can be only one faith, and one interpretation of the Truth."
~ Saint Liberatus

The Great Schism and other disputes about doctrine raise the question about how we know what the truth is. Today there are thousands of competing claims to different truths about God and the nature of the Church and it is understandable that many people are confused or deceived on these matters. When the Jehovah's Witnesses turn up at the door few people are equipped to recognise the false assumptions on which the visitors base their arguments and when random Old Testament quotations are thrown at us it is easy to lose track of what is being proposed or defended.

In fact the Church bases the authority of its teaching on three sources: the Ecumenical Councils, Holy Tradition and the Bible and we shall now consider each in turn.

As time passed from the first generation of Christians, false ideas (heresies) began to appear which were clearly at odds with the teaching of Christ and the Apostles. From the earliest times the Church always settled disputes by reaching a consensus of opinion in a council. In fact the very first of these appears in the fifteenth chapter of the Book of Acts when it was necessary to decide to what degree the Gentiles joining the Church should be expected to be obedient to the rules of the Jewish Law of Moses. This practice continued at every level of the Church's life, both at the local and universal level. Bishops were not only encouraged but required by Church law to meet regularly in councils.

While local councils could resolve issues relating to the governance of dioceses, matters of doctrine required the whole Church to be in agreement. But such major meetings were only necessary when heresies were threatening to mislead large groups of Christians. At these times councils were called not to create doctrine but to find appropriate ways of expressing what the Church believed in order to nullify the particular heresy being faced. There have been seven of these major councils which have expressed the mind of the Church and each was called by an emperor and to them were invited all the bishops of the Church (though the realities of distance meant some of the councils were attended by relatively few). The Seven Ecumenical Councils defined dogmas but also created Canon laws which were rules for the conduct of life within the Church. Let us consider each of the seven and identify the teaching that was proclaimed in them.

The First Ecumenical Council (325 A.D.) was called by Emperor Constantine in Nicea to deal with the teachings of a priest called Arius. His heresy, known as Arianism, was to claim that Christ is not the pre-eternal uncreated Second Person of the Holy Trinity. The council created the first seven sections of the Nicene Creed which expressed faith in Christ as true God, of One Essence with the Father. Arianism was condemned and Orthodoxy upheld. There were 318 bishops and a number of great saints at this council (including Saint Spyridon whose body remains incorrupt in Corfu and Saint Nicholas the Wonder-worker) and as in the following councils, many miraculous signs and healings were witnessed. The council also set the date for Pascha and declared that priests should not be required to be celibate.

The Second Ecumenical Council (381 A.D.) was called by Emperor Theodosius in Constantinople. At this time a bishop, Macedonius, who had accepted Arian teaching was denying the divinity of the Holy Spirit as the Third person of the Holy Trinity. In response the council produced the second section of the Creed which proclaims the Holy Spirit as being of one essence with the Father and the Son as well as the final clauses regarding the Church and the final judgement. At this council the 150 bishops included Gregory the Theologian and Gregory of Nyssa.

The Third Ecumenical Council (431 A.D.) was called in Ephesus by Emperor Theodosius II. This council was in response to Nestorius (who was then Archbishop of Constantinople) who was teaching that the Virgin Mary only gave birth to Jesus the man within whom God then dwelled just as He had in the prophets of the Old Testament. Nestorius taught that Christ should not be called God incarnate but God-bearing. The rejection of this heresy resulted in the recognition of the Virgin Mary as truly *Mother of God* (Theotokos) and not just *Mother of Christ* (Christotokos). Christ was declared to have two natures, one divine one human, making Him truly and fully God and truly and fully man. At this council the 200 bishops also prohibited any changes to the wording of the Creed.

The Fourth Ecumenical Council (451 A.D.) was convened in Chalcedon by the Emperor Marcian. Whereas previous heresies had taught that Christ or the Holy Spirit were not fully divine, the Church was now dealing with a monk called Eutychius who was claiming that Christ was not truly human. His intention had been to proclaim the divinity of Christ but his thinking led him to teach that Christ's humanity was somehow absorbed into His divinity: the teaching became known as Monophysitism and was rejected by the 650 bishops present. The Church recognised that in the One person of Christ the two natures exist and are indivisible.

The Fifth Ecumenical Council (553 A.D.) was called by the Emperor Justinian I in Constantinople. A dispute had arisen between Nestorians and Monophysites and the 165 bishops in attendance reconfirmed faith in the Holy Trinity and in Christ's true identity as God's only begotten Son.

The Sixth Ecumenical Council (680 A.D.) was convened in Constantinople by Emperor Constantine IV. Though the doctrine of the two natures of Christ was not being contested, heretics were now claiming that though fully human Christ could only have one divine will. The great hero of this council was Saint Maximos the Confessor (who died before the council but whose teaching was declared by those present) who had carried in his body terrible scars from persecution (including having had his tongue cut out). This gave his teaching great authority at the council and the 170 bishops confirmed that Christ has two wills but that the human will submits itself to the divine. The bishops, as well as a Roman delegation, also condemned Pope Honorius for his acceptance of the heresy of one will. The council also formulated the canons by which the Church would be governed, often called "The Rudder" which would be added to at the next council.

The Seventh Ecumenical Council (787 A.D.) was called by the Empress Irene in Nicea like the first. At this time the Church was facing what is known as the iconoclast heresy which consisted of a rejection of the use of holy icons. The dispute had lasted sixty years and many scholars argue that it was under the pressure of Muslims that many Church leaders succumbed to it. The council proclaimed not only that the veneration of icons should be permitted but that it is a necessary expression of our faith and subsequently the triumph of Orthodoxy is celebrated on the first Sunday of Great Lent.

The decisions of these councils were universally accepted throughout the Church and today only the Orthodox Church continues to defend and live according to them. There have subsequently been many local councils which have been expressions of the consciousness of the Church but they are primarily concerned with ethical and ecclesiastical matters. But for the Church there are only seven councils and no pan-Orthodox gathering has ever equalled their scope or standing.

Holy Tradition

The term "dogmatic" has become something of a slur in modern use: it implies rigidity and a lack of openness to new ideas of the day. This mindset must be rejected completely when we approach the term *dogma* in the way it is used in the Church. As

God has revealed Himself to the Church through Christ and the Holy Spirit the Church has expressed these truths as *dogmas*. Their fixed nature is a reflection of their eternal reality which is at odds with the fashions of man's worldly thinking. In the twenty-first century we see social attitudes changing at an increasing rate and people's language and attitudes quickly become outdated. But despite this chaotic swirl that dominates the world's thinking the Church has not only defined but protected the rock of faith that remains unmoved as the waves of uncertainty break upon it. The Ecumenical Councils took as their guides the sacred tradition of the Church and the Holy Scriptures.

Holy Tradition came into existence during the time of the Apostles, it was that inner life of the Church that was guarded from the world when persecution and rejection was commonplace for Christians. For example the rites of Baptism and Holy Communion were not at first recorded in written form and indeed non-Christians were not permitted to attend baptisms or that part of the Eucharistic service that followed the service of the Word. The patterns of the services were passed on orally and were not to be revealed to those who did not seek salvation in Christ. We might recognise here the fact that the word *mystery* is frequently used amongst early Church writers not just to express the theological reality of *mysterion*, the action of God which is beyond rational thought, but also the life of the Church that remained hidden to those outside of Christ's Body. We therefore recognise as our starting point that Holy Tradition is called *Apostolic* because it was delivered by the Fathers but it is also called *ecclesiastic* because each generation of the Church in turn received it and passed it on to the next.

We read in Saint Basil the Great: *Of the dogmas and sermons preserved in the Church, certain ones we have from written instruction, and certain ones we have received from the Apostolic Tradition, handed down in secret.* We find this view amongst all the Church Fathers and also expressed at the Ecumenical Councils: the existence of the oral tradition within the Church was recognised as an essential element in the *Catholic Consciousness* of the Church. As the Church was released from periods of persecution this tradition was written down and shared in recognition that it was the living experience of Christians. This recording was not an invention of new rules or rites but a reflection of what already existed and can be found in a number of places: in the services of the Church; in the Canons of the Holy Apostles; in the Creeds; in the various written accounts of the Church's history and in the writings of the Church Fathers.

The Church has defended this Tradition against heresy through the councils described above because the very life and spirit of the Church is found in the Sacred Tradition which belongs to the whole Church and not just to the hierarchy or theologians. It is the personal experience of every member of the Church and the heresies which have attacked it have therefore been attacks on the living reality of what it means to belong to Christ. Street riots have erupted over heretical teachings, Arianism resulted in pitched battles where many people lost their lives on both sides because people not only understood the importance of what was at stake they also felt the impact of heresy on their daily lives.

Holy Tradition is the only means by which Holy Scripture can be properly understood. If we remove the Bible from the life of the Church it becomes possible to interpret verses in a multitude of different ways resulting today in the countless Protestant groups who all claim to have been inspired by the Holy Spirit to find the correct interpretation. It was from Sacred Tradition that the Sacred Scriptures were born: from the shared life of the Church the bishops were able to identify which texts would form the New Testament.

We should also note that there are many revealed truths that are simply not recorded in the Bible while others are easily misunderstood without the guidance of Holy Tradition. This leads us to the other source of authority within the Church: Holy Scripture.

We should ask ourselves what the Church's view of the Bible is and why this is important. In Islam the Qur'an is seen as a recording of the literal words of God recited by a man just as they were revealed to him and in recent years some Christians have attempted to impose this same approach on Sacred Scripture. Other liberal academics have gone to the opposite extreme and have argued that the Bible is an expression of concerns from a particular set of historical circumstances and has little relevance to modern man. Both of these approaches are in error and are not the way the early Church or the Church through the centuries viewed the texts. It will be useful to first consider how we should approach the texts, how the canon of Holy Scripture came about, which versions we should read and then we will present the Orthodox response to the Protestant heresy of *Sola Scriptura*.

It has often been said that the Church does not simply read Holy Scripture it prays it. We do this not as separated individuals but collectively as the Body of Christ. Therefore how Holy Scripture is used within the life of the Church should reveal to us its message and nature: just as we encounter Christ in our worship so we should see the Holy Scriptures as a means to drawing closer to God within the life of the Body. Just as we should devote time and effort to preparing ourselves for worship, so it is important to ask God to help us as we read the words of Holy Scripture. A simple prayer such as *Holy God, fill my heart and mind with your grace and illuminate me with the truth and life of your Holy Scripture* is appropriate. Of course it is important that we approach Holy Scripture with the intention of receiving it, that is that we will act on what God gives us and that we will allow Him to change us and instruct us in how to live properly. In this sense we do not simply read it but live it.

We should recognise the words of Christ as being truly the words of God. In His eternal wisdom God has spoken to all men in all ages and we must accept Christ's words as though they were spoken directly to us. We receive Christ's words in the New Testament as personal and specific, they have the power to heal and save as much as they did when they were first uttered. Christ Himself assured us *Heaven and earth will pass away, but my words will not pass away* (Mat. 24 v35).

One of the features of many Protestant places of worship is a huge volume of the Bible, normally with a black cover, that sits in a prominent position in front of the pews. It may therefore come as a surprise to many converts that the early Church did not produce a single volume like this and indeed in many Orthodox churches today you will often have to ask to find a copy. Before alarm bells start ringing in some people's heads we should look more closely at what has happened through history. In fact the early Church used many books, in the beginning these were in scroll form and today sections of the Bible appear in different service books. For example the Gospels are kept on the Holy Altar, usually in a large and decorated form. This volume is venerated with incense and is kissed by clergy during the services as a sign of its importance. The Epistles appear in a separate volume called the Apostolos and other sections of the Holy Scriptures appear elsewhere. The Orthodox tradition of using the texts in this way reflects what was done in those first centuries of the Church and since the liturgical practice has captured the way they were used, we find ourselves today with these different books. Only when the printing press had been invented did it become normal practice amongst many Christian groups to have a single volume bringing the texts together. This may be useful in the home but not for worship based on the ancient practices of the Church.

The final canon of scripture, that is the list of which books should be included, came into existence through a process rather than in a single moment. We should first note that the Church is not based on the Bible but rather the Church produced the Bible. In the early Church there were many documents copied and shared amongst different local churches for use in worship. There was some disagreement about which texts were genuine and also about how useful or edifying texts were and it was recognised that an authoritative canon was necessary in order to maintain good order but also so that the shared Catholic Consciousness would be reflected by the texts. A number of attempts were made at producing a definitive list over a number of centuries but it was in 393 A.D in Hippo and again in 397 A.D. in Carthage that the list we have today of twenty-seven books was first drawn up and later ratified by Ecumenical Councils: but we should recognise that the canon was already in effect ratified by the shared usage within the Church

The canon of the Old Testament is more problematic in some ways, though not for the Orthodox. During the Reformation some Protestants took issue with particular texts, especially those which supported the position of the Theotokos, and so removed books from the Old Testament. In Jewish practice at the time of Christ there had been two versions of the Scriptures, known as the *Narrow Circle* of Jerusalem and the *Wider Circle* of Alexandria: the latter is known as the *Septuagint* (coming from the word for seventy because seventy-two independent scholars produced and agreed its content). Christ, the Apostles and the early Church all used the *Septuagint* which was written in Greek.

In fact the *Septuagint* presented three main difficulties for Protestants and Jews which resulted in the removal of certain texts. First the Jews wanted all clear prophesy of Christ's Messiahship removed and so the books known as Apocrypha posed a problem. Second the role of the Theotokos in these books was an issue for both Jews and Protestants and finally the references to prayers offered for the dead were at odds with Protestants who had abandoned the ancient practice and with it the true understanding of the Church united in Heaven and on earth. It is very important to note that both the Apostles and the early Church writers made numerous references to the *Septuagint* which had different wording and meaning to the Hebrew version. In 100 A.D, Jewish scholars removed many of the prophecies about Christ in a Hebrew translation. At the Reformation when the texts were being translated into different languages the academics mistakenly assumed that the Hebrew version must pre-date the Greek since Hebrew is the language of the Jews. And so today almost all Protestants use an incomplete and butchered version of the Holy Scriptures. If we are looking for an English translation that best reflects the Septuagint we should look to the King James version despite its somewhat archaic language.

It should be noted too that many so-called modern biblical scholars adopt an atheistic stance on the texts. As a result they will often seek to reduce the strength of language proclaiming Christ as God and even well respected translations like the Revised Standard Version (RSV) have blatant alterations which act against Christian faith. For example the RSV uses a mixture of *thou, thee, you and he.* In this way God is addressed as *thou* but Christ and all others are addressed as *you.* The

RSV does address Christ as *Thou* once He has ascended but we can see the subtle message at work. There are multiple examples where the RSV removes references to Christ as the Son of God and Lord: in short my advice to those seeking the authentic scriptures is to avoid these Protestant versions as they present a warped theology that diminishes Christ's divinity.

One further example of the Protestant bias in these translations is the way *tradition* is presented. The Greek word for *teachings* is translated as such when it is used in a positive manner, but each time it appears in a negative way, for example when Christ is confronting the Pharisees, the translators insert the word *tradition* instead. The ignorant reader will then form a false sense of what the scriptures are teaching. Many Protestant translations use this trick including the NIV.

The Church interprets the whole of Holy Scripture, Old and New Testaments, in terms of Christ. Everything we find there finds its meaning in Him. The Old Testament is a kind of preparation for His coming and we find many events and people in the time of Christ prefigured in the Old Testament. Orthodox scholars have approached the texts with a critical enquiry, but always it is done with hearts filled with faith: we study writings not just of human authors but genuinely inspired by God. But we must recognise that many parts of the Bible are not obviously understood with a casual reading, in fact it is all too easy for us to project our own thinking into what we find there and make interpretations more reflective of our own psychology than of the divinely inspired truth. The Holy Scriptures do not come to us without guidance. The Church Fathers wrote copious volumes on how to make sense of these ancient texts, and though passages have the power to speak to us at times in personal and specific ways, we also need the assistance of the Church from which these texts came. Rejecting this approach has been at the heart of the Protestant error and we will now focus more closely on this issue of interpretation and how the Reformation thinkers made a fatal mistake.

Let us first paint with broad strokes a simple picture of how the error occurred. The Protestants recognised the error of the false claim of Rome about the Pope being the supreme authority over matters of doctrine. They rightly saw no support for this in Holy Scripture or the early Church. But in rejecting the one false authority they mistakenly adopted a different single authority to replace the first. The very mindset of the Reformation was still so deeply influenced by Latin thinking that they rejected one error only to replace it with another. Not knowing or understanding the history of the Church and the reality of Orthodoxy, the Reformers could only see the Patriarchate of Rome as being the Church which they longed to change, and so they failed to recognise the importance and place of Tradition. To the Protestant thinkers

Tradition was nothing more than the distorted practices of a corrupt papacy with which they wanted no part. They had been taught a false understanding of the Great Schism by a papal system desperate to maintain its claims to being both supreme head of the Church but also a genuine part of the One True Church. With five hundred years of papal propaganda at work it shouldn't come as a surprise that the Protestants failed at the first hurdle.

The heresy of *Sola Scriptura* essentially teaches that Christians will find everything they need to know in the Bible in order to be saved. Tradition is seen as something separate and additional to scripture and unnecessary for us. This argument is filled with contradiction and error. Even the Holy Scriptures themselves teach that this is not true but there are wider arguments too.

First let us deal with what the authors of the biblical texts themselves said about Tradition. There are many examples we could use, let us begin with Saint Paul's instruction in his second letter to the church in Thessalonica (which still exists today):

Therefore brethren, stand fast, and hold the traditions which you have been taught, whether by word or our epistle (2 Thes. 3 v6). Here Saint Paul refers to the oral tradition as well as the written text which would enter the canon of the New Testament.

Again in verse six of chapter three of the same letter he writes:

In the name of the Lord Jesus Christ, we command you brothers, to keep away from every brother who is idle and does not live according to the tradition you have received from us.

One more example is in the Second Letter to Timothy where Saint Paul writes:

And the things you have heard me say in the presence of many witnesses entrust to reliable men who will also be qualified to teach others. The first bishops, the Apostles, did exactly this when they appointed those who would follow them in safeguarding these oral traditions. At the end of the second century we find Saint Irenaeus confirming that this practice was to be found in the life of the early Church when he writes:

We refer them to that tradition which originates from the Apostles which is preserved by means of the succession of presbyters in the churches.

We should remember that Irenaeus was a disciple of Saint Polycarp who himself had been taught directly by the Apostle John. This is not some later addition but comes from the very beginning of the Church's existence. To argue against the place of Tradition within the life of the Church is to abandon the very foundations put in place by the Apostles.

But if the Holy Scriptures themselves are not enough to make the point let us reflect on the place of Holy Scripture within Holy Tradition. The fact is the two are not separate, Holy Tradition encompasses the biblical texts: the proper order of worship and the inner structure of the Church was established and passed on by the Apostles along with their writings. And it is from within this Tradition that the canon of Scripture was established. The books of the New Testament were accepted or rejected according to their reflection and agreement of the existing traditions of the Church. If Protestant thinkers reject the developing life of the Church during the first four centuries they are also rejecting the process which gave us the New Testament. The Holy Spirit guided the Church Fathers in their selection of texts but also in their defence and maintenance of the Tradition passed on to them from the Apostles. It is contradictory to suggest that they were only listening to the Holy Spirit over the one issue and not the other.

Sola Scriptura maintains that Holy Scripture is sufficient in and of itself for interpretation; that the meaning is sufficiently clear within the whole text for no other means of interpretation to be necessary. If this were the case we might ask how and why thousands upon thousands of rival Protestant groups have appeared, each with their own correct interpretation of the Bible. Some argue for infant baptism, some only for adults, some argue for a real presence in the Eucharist while others say it is symbolic. Some acknowledge a priesthood while others reject it. The list goes on, and to support their claims the different groups quote various snippets of the Bible. In fact we see this process beginning within a decade of the Reformation starting: the Orthodox Church has maintained its unity of doctrine for two thousand years while the Protestant Reformers managed it for ten years! Their very approach to scripture is flawed and is the cause of further disunity.

At the root of this problem for Protestants is the idea that each Christian is free to interpret the Holy Scriptures *as the spirit guides them*. Clearly they are coming to opposing conclusions and we must ask which spirit is doing the guiding: it certainly is not the Holy Spirit that proceeds from the Father. Their reaction against the authority of the Pope and the magisterium set up to interpret the Holy Scripture and produce doctrine is understandable, but the confusion over Tradition led them to this individualised approach to the text. It has been said that Protestantism sets up each and every man as his own Pope, free to interpret the Bible as he will. At best this displays a terrible lack of humility and at worst assumes a spiritual maturity few in the modern world truly possess. The danger is that Holy Scripture can be misinterpreted so as to lead people to commit evil. This sounds as though I am overstating the case but we must remember Christ's experience in the wilderness. After tempting Him twice Satan then used teachings from the Old Testament in order to get Christ to sin: "It is written…" The text can be bent out of shape and its message abused when individual lines are taken out of context, and the context for the whole of Holy Scripture is Holy Tradition. Many parts of the Bible are extremely difficult to understand, their complexity is part of the text's richness. However much Protestants try to compare texts and use the one to explain the other, they ultimately fall back on their own presumptions to reach an interpretation since they have abandoned the clear path set out in Tradition.

The Church's teaching is that everything in Holy Tradition must always conform with the Holy Scriptures. The New Testament is a part of this Tradition but not its entirety. The life of the Church is filled with the presence of the Holy Spirit and it is from this experience that Holy Tradition developed. Today we see the Holy Scriptures used throughout the services of the Orthodox Church, almost every line of the Divine Liturgy is filled with biblical references. While many Protestants ignore the writings of the Church Fathers and fill their bookshelves with paperbacks from the last one hundred years, Orthodoxy is filled with the voices of the very earliest Christians who knew and were in communion with the Apostles. The same life that characterised the early Church is experienced in Orthodoxy today and continues to be filled with God's presence. While rejecting *sola scriptura,* the Orthodox Church sees the Holy Scriptures as an essential part of this continuing life which is why we see it as vital to interpret them correctly.

We will now turn our attention to how the Church does not demand rigid application of its rules before moving on to the inner life of the Church and focus on its worship.

Economia

"As a handful of sand thrown into the ocean, so are the sins of all flesh as compared with the mind of God."
~ Saint Isaac The Syrian

There are times when bishops will permit things to take place which appear to contravene canon law: this is called *economy* (from the Greek *economia*). To understand the principle behind this let us use an example. Canon law prohibits weddings during Great Lent because it is a time of repentance and the joy of a wedding service would be inappropriate. But a soldier approaches his bishop and says he has been called to the front line and believes his life is likely to be in danger. Before he leaves he wishes to marry the woman he loves and asks for a blessing. Under these circumstances the bishop may decide that it is right to allow the couple to marry, even in Lent. Similarly many Orthodox may have found themselves as guests in the homes of friends on a Friday and at dinner may be served meat. In such circumstances it would be unacceptable to reject the hospitality of their host and so they have justifiably broken the fasting rules of the Church.

In both cases Orthodox Christians recognise a

form of discretion which can be applied which we call *economy*. The first point to make about this is that we must not try to fully define what is meant by *economy* since we believe it is an expression of the mysteries of God's mercy and our salvation: we cannot apply legalistic concepts to God's infinite mercy and love. The authority to make such decisions comes from Christ (Mat 16 v19) and is a canonical power to overcome anything that might act as a hindrance to salvation. If a bishop believes that an individual's salvation or peace in a community may be furthered by such use of *economy* then he is able to do so as long as he is in no way acting against Church dogma: this is an absolutely crucial point to understand.

We do not see such actions as breaking or working against canon law, instead they are understood to be in accordance with the spirit of the law even if the appearance is of an exception to the norm. Canon law exists to maintain good order and enable our salvation and so such uses of *economy* are in keeping with their ultimate purpose.

Orthodoxy understands there to be two principles with regards to canon law: *economia* and *akribeia.* This second term refers to exactness or strictness in application of the law. Such an approach is to be found on Mount Athos but even here we find *economia* at work: the rule of only giving Holy Communion to those baptised as Orthodox is not always applied as I know of at least one English bishop who was received into Orthodoxy through chrismation only and is still given full ecclesiastical honours when he visits the Holy Mountain. But *economia* and *akribeia* should be seen as true and full manifestations of Orthodoxy, both are necessary for there to be a balance within the life of the Church. We are not dealing with legal formulations but the living experience of Orthodox reality and so what may appear superficially as a contradiction is in fact the full expression of life in the Holy Spirit. *Economia* is not a rejection of strictness, it is not a desire to get around the rules of the Church, but is the manifestation of their inner spirit.

Economia in Greek refers to *good management* and is applied to God's management of our world and of ecclesiastical management of the Church. *Divine economia* is seen at work through God's willingness to forgive sinners for whom justice would require punishment. Instead God sends His Son and then His Holy Spirit in order that we might be saved. In our prayers we ask God to forgive our many sins and yet we go on sinning: but God does not remove His mercy. This principle is at work in ecclesiastical use of economy, it is the Church's participation in God's love, an understanding that the intention or purpose of the law is greater and higher than the letter of the law. But such action does not set a precedent for the future; each use of economy is a unique case which has no effect on any further circumstances.

We should understand *economia* as a theological rather than legal principle. Christ is a living symbol of its meaning, His willingness to be incarnate and then mix and eat with sinners calls us to view the world with the same compassion and forgiveness. We must see the reality of people before us as they are in each moment and not judge according to preconceived ideas. Canon law is in no way undermined by such an approach, rather God's presence within it is made more clear when we know we are each treated as the unique individuals we are by both the Church and God.

What Is Worship?

"We are commanded to worship, not on special days, but continuously, all our life through, and in all possible ways."
~ Saint Clement of Alexandria

To understand the purpose and place of worship within the Orthodox Church we need to first recognise that the services are themselves a part of Holy Tradition. We worship God in our services but we also learn about Him and our faith. We learn about how He has revealed Himself to others and we have presented to us the responses of saintly people who have shared their experiences of His intervention in their lives. But we also need to see the Church's worship in the context of Jewish worship before it. We will first reflect on worship itself before looking at specific services and aspects of worship which should help us to experience it more deeply.

The word for liturgy comes from the Greek word *leitourgia* which expresses the idea of the services being the *work of the people*. Worship is a common act in which all present participate. The congregation is not an audience passively watching what the priest does; the congregation is an active participant necessary for the service to take place. The words of the priest express the faith of the people present, he faces east because he speaks to God with and for the people: the western practice of clergy facing the congregation denies this important truth since he or she speaks to the congregation. The people present are expected to participate through the singing of hymns and by expressing *Amen* at the end of prayers. Even the ritual actions of the congregation such as making the sign of the cross or bowing (which will be discussed in more detail later) are actions which confirm agreement and participation in what is happening in the service. This is why it has been the Church's custom whenever possible to conduct services in the languages of the people: in many western congregations where people speak a variety of languages there are often parts of services spoken or sung in different languages for the sake of these people. In the parish I serve it is the custom for the Lord's Prayer to be recited in turn in each of the languages used by members of the congregation which creates a powerful sense of the universality of our faith.

If we look for the very core of what makes Orthodoxy what it is, we find worship. Worship is the true heart and nature of God's Church and it can be described as having two principle aspects: the way we encounter God and the unity of God's people. The first aspect concerns the way God reveals or manifests Himself in the life of human beings. Although we can see worship as consisting of words sung and spoken by people it is in its truest sense a gift from God. But it is also the presence and power of the Holy Spirit that makes human worship of God possible. When we are drawn closer to God it is God who makes this happen; our worship is the means by which we allow ourselves to be made aware of what God is doing.

But simultaneously worship is also an offering which the Church makes to God. As He brings His people together we not only recognise and experience God in our midst but we do so together: our praise and thanksgiving is offered not from disparate individuals but collectively as a Body. We are drawn closer to one another within the Church through our worship. A further dimension of this is that Orthodoxy sees the drawing of all humanity into this worship of God as a missionary act: the beauty and wonder of Orthodox worship has enabled many people outside the Church to seek its inner experience.

Some Christians today imagine that the worship of the early Church must have been unstructured but in fact it was highly liturgical. Our services today follow a prescribed order for a number of reasons not least of which is because this is the way the Apostles and others worshipped. By following a set pattern in our worship we maintain continuity with the early Church and we also protect the teaching aspect of worship and ensure that the words reflect the true faith of Christ. But the liturgical nature of our worship also ensures that the corporate nature of our worship is protected. I recall being in a church on Mount Athos and despite my very limited language skills I knew exactly where we were as the service progressed because its underlying pattern and ritual actions were familiar. Each congregation is assured that its worship isn't the result of fashion or the priest's personal preferences, but is a local expression of the same action performed through out the world.

This leads us to an important point: the early Church's worship was liturgical because the first Christians (the Apostles) were Jewish. The Church's worship reflects the worship in the Temple in Jerusalem. The Apostles understood that collective encounter of God is to be found in liturgical worship and this is what we find throughout the Holy Scriptures (Old and New Testament). The early Church followed a specific pattern in its worship and until the Reformation this was the case everywhere in the world. Today we see many musical forms of Christian worship still have their roots in these Jewish origins, such as the chanting of Psalms and the role of a priesthood. Scholars demonstrate that within around three decades the completely Jewish character of the Church's worship had been influenced by Greek forms and as the faith spread, so other national musical styles and traditions influenced local practice. Most notably, the legalisation of

Christianity in the Roman Empire in the fourth century allowed the development of what became known as the Byzantine style of music which had and continues to have such an enormous impact on the Church.

The fact that the first Christians were Jews raises a further point with regards to worship: the Sabbath. Seventh Day Adventists today consider worship on a Sunday to be an abandonment of the Law of Moses and a sign of apostasy. But when we look at the reality we see something different. We know from early Christian writings that many in the Church observed two Sabbaths: the first reflected the Jewish practice (Friday into Saturday) and the second was when they met for Holy Communion on the day of the Resurrection (Sunday). Our idea of the beginning and ending of a day is different to that of the early Church. The Jewish Sabbath began at the appearance of stars in the sky on Friday and ended at the same time on Saturday. What we now see as the evening was recognised as the beginning of the following day. The liturgical rhythm of the Church continues to reflect this: vespers in the evening will focus on the theme of the following day. On Mount Athos it is not just the liturgical pattern that reflects this understanding of the day but every aspect of life. Therefore when the Apostles met on Saturday evening to celebrate Holy Communion it was to them the Day of the Resurrection.

But a further development occurred. While Christians could at first mix with Jews in the Temple, toleration of them did not last long. Even in the twenty-first chapter of the Book of Acts we read of the violent reaction to Saint Paul's presence in the Temple grounds. The first wave of persecution of Christians came from the Jews and with it came exclusion from the Temple and synagogues. This exclusion quickly separated the Christians from the Jewish community even before gentiles were joining the Church in any great numbers. Perhaps inevitably we see the early Church just as quickly abandoning its observance of the Jewish Sabbath in favour of a single collective worship on Sundays. In fact the persecution by Jews was really only part of the story. The Eucharist was never something that could be added to Jewish worship and would never have been permitted within synagogues even if the Jews had not begun killing Christians.

The developing sense of Christian identity as more than a Jewish sect was not the whole story however, Judaism itself was about to be radically changed. The destruction of the Temple in 70 A.D. by the Romans forced Jews to create new forms of worship beyond the sacrificial system that was at its heart. During the following three centuries the emergence of rabbinic Judaism which was heavily influenced by the Babylonian Talmud would transform the faith into nothing that was truly reflective of what had taken place in the Temple.

Whereas the Christian emphasis on the sacrifice of Christ as the Lamb of God was not something that replaced the practice of the Temple but which fulfilled it: Jewish worship had abandoned its Old Testament forms. With the destruction of the Temple it was Christian worship which was the genuine successor to Temple practice while the synagogue system was a far more pluralistic approach which reflected the many cultures and religious practices which had found their way into Jewish life as a result of the diaspora. Judaism was made up of two very different traditions: that in Jerusalem and that in Babylon. The Roman action against the former meant the latter was able to attain dominance resulting in the foundations of modern Judaism which is so different from the faith of Christ. While American Baptists continue to proclaim support for Israel and the Jewish people, what they fail to understand is that the religion they are supporting is not the one found in the Old Testament: it emerged after the time of Christ.

Christian worship is a reflection of the eternal worship offered in Heaven. The Old Testament gave clear guidance on what this worship is like and the Temple practices were patterned after it. Therefore when Christians come together to worship God they should be aware of what they are doing as both reflecting but also joining the heavenly worship. Behind the altar we have fans depicting the cherubim as a reminder both of the golden angels which Moses was instructed to have placed beside the Ark of the Covenant but also that our earthly altars transcend the limits of time and space to join the angelic worship: and so we remind ourselves too of the angels that surround our earthly altars.

The early Christians lived with an expectation of Christ's return within their lifetime. As the Church began to understand its role within time it recognised the need to develop a pattern of festivals and seasons to guide the faithful through their lives. This is often referred to as the *sanctification of time* since the passing of days, weeks and months were given a spiritual dimension that supported worship of God. But in the calendar we once again find elements of Jewish practice. We should first recognise that there were two aspects to Jewish worship which happened in different places. The Temple was the focus, for most Jews, only on certain days of the year as it was the place for sacrifice which had to be offered on specific festivals. For the majority of the time there was a cycle of prayers and meals which followed daily, weekly and monthly patterns. Even before 70 A.D. the synagogue had its place within Jewish life but its context was within a faith that still had the Temple sacrifices and all the messianic expectations that went along with it. The Temple was an essential element; it was not something in addition to the other practices. When Rome destroyed the Temple it also destroyed the possibility of true Jewish worship. Sacrifices could only be offered in that one place in the Holy City and without sacrifice the basis of worship was gone. As we shall see, for the Christians sacrifice was equally important but found its meaning in Christ: the repetition of animal sacrifices was completed in Christ and every hope and anticipation that was read in the words of the prophets had become a reality.

Having considered worship in general we will now focus our attention on specific services and sacraments. But before doing so it is important to remember that no matter how much we read about worship a true understanding can only be gained through experience. Worship is full of mystery which cannot be rationalised but only experienced in the heart. Therefore for anyone enquiring about Orthodoxy I would say first go and attend the services and taste the flavour and traditions for yourself.

The Sacraments

"If you did not have a body these bodiless gifts would be given to you starkly but because the soul is interwoven with the body, the Divine Life is transmitted to you in visible things such as water and oil."
~ Saint John Chrysostom

Before we look at some of the particular sacraments we should stop to consider what we mean by sacraments in general. First we should note that the Orthodox Church does not apply a rigid definition of what is meant by a sacrament and so does not limit what is considered a sacrament to a specific number. There are seven major sacraments (if we can use that term) but also many other forms of prayer, blessing and sacred actions which have a sacramental quality. This is because the Church is recognised as being a sacramental Body and so its presence and role in human life cannot be reduced to a few specific examples.

The Church's understanding of the sacraments comes from the effect and consequences of Christ's Incarnation. By becoming man He entered into the physical cosmos and so changed it. It is not just man's relation to God which Christ changed but the whole created order now has a different purpose and value. Physical matter is not considered evil or something to transcend but is a means to knowing God. The creation was realigned to God through Christ's Incarnation and so is able to play its part in our salvation. Many of the sacraments use physical substances like wine, bread, oil and water as outward signs of what God is doing in the sacrament. And in this way the Church draws the physical universe up into its worship of God rather than trying to escape from it as is taught in Hinduism (and which has entered the thinking of some heterodox groups).

The Church teaches that the sacraments have a dual effect: they enable us to experience God by first making Him known to us and secondly by changing us so that we are able to receive Him. God acts in the sacraments, they are a means of revelation, but as we are united with Christ we are also changed further into His likeness; the Church calls this process *theosis*.

We believe in a God Who is not distant, He draws near to us and wants us to experience Him. The whole of creation is filled with His life and presence: Saint Justin Martyr called this *logos spermadicos*, which means God poured Himself out into every part of the universe. But in our sinful state we turn away from God, we refuse His love and we shut ourselves off from His life. In His infinite love God then went further and gave specific ways for us to discover all that we have turned away from. In the sacraments God strengthens and guides us, He cleanses and unites us to Himself and to one another. The sacraments are a necessary means of healing and restoration of our whole being.

The Church teaches that we are saved by God in every way, in soul and body. Just as the created order plays its part in our salvation so our own bodies are not only to be resurrected but are a vital part of the process of our salvation. Many of the sacraments involve something being done to the body as a sign of this truth, for example anointing with oil or washing in water.

Instead of calling these actions sacraments the Church has often referred to them as *mysteries*. Saint Thomas Aquinas used Augustine's ideas to formulate very exact ideas of what is necessary to constitute what they called *valid* sacraments. These legalistic ideas resulted in the false belief that so long as water is used for example with the correct formula of words then a baptism has taken place regardless of the faith or context of those involved: whether they are heretics or even Muslims or Jews. The Orthodox Church rejects this approach entirely. We do not see the sacraments as being a mechanistic process like a spell or formula. In fact the Church has avoided identifying specific points in services where God is understood to act but instead recognises the importance of the whole rite, the fullness of the prayers and ritual actions as a single action within which God meets with us.

These ideas will be developed further as we look at some of the sacraments and explore their meaning and function within the life of the Church.

Baptism and Chrismation

"Our head is plunged in the water as in a tomb. The old man is buried and completely drowned. When we emerge from the water the new man is raised from the dead."
~ Saint John Chrysostom

Let us look at baptism and chrismation together so that we understand them as part of a single process. We will look at why it is an error to separate them by first looking at the practice of the first Christians.

In the first century it took a long time to become part of the Church. A period of preparation could last at least a year during which those seeking baptism were called *catechumens*. When it came to the rite itself it always consisted of two parts: the immersion into water and the anointing with oil. The service had a unity; it was not two separate events forced together. There are theological reasons for this which will become clear and it is important to understand baptism and chrismation in this way.

Baptism and chrismation are the means by which we become part of the Church, they mark our entrance to the Church. It is a sacramental act which cannot be replaced with an individualised expression of faith that is today described by so-called born-again Christians. Personal faith is very important and necessary in adults, but it is not the whole story. For some Protestants it is the personal declaration of faith that is important and the baptism acts as a kind of public acknowledgement of what the believer is professing. This does not reflect the Church's understanding. In baptism we believe that God acts on us, the font is represented as a womb from which a new person emerges (born again). The cleansing of baptism is a reality, in it God washes us clean of our sins, and as Saint Paul says we *put on Christ* (Gal.3 v27).

From the very beginning the Church baptised by immersing people three times in the name of the Holy Trinity. The water symbolises the soil of the grave and as the person goes down and then is lifted up out of the water we see enacted a great symbol of resurrection. But while this is essential there is more needed. Many times in the New Testament we hear Christ promising to send us the Holy Spirit and without the descent of the Holy Spirit the action is incomplete. We are cleansed in the baptismal water but we are not yet filled with the Holy Spirit. Tertullian wrote in the third century that the waters of baptism prepare us for the Holy Spirit, in other words we need to be released from our sins before the Holy Spirit will enter us. We must be cleansed of our impurity before coming into union with God's holiness.

After cleansing the candidate is anointed with the oil of chrism and receives spiritual strength and nourishment, God gives His grace in a unique way: both baptism and chrismation can only ever be performed once in a person's life. The oil is applied to specific parts of the body in order to strengthen the candidate for their life in Christ: the forehead to sanctify the mind, the chest for the heart, the eyes, ears and lips to sanctify the senses and finally the hands and feet to sanctify the person's works and to maintain them on the path of salvation. This is also a further example of how the Church understands salvation as involving the whole person.

The practice of using oil in this way has a number of reasons. First it is a continuation of Jewish practice: whenever anyone was chosen to be a king or some other role they were anointed with oil as a sign of the seal of God on them. The oil confirmed God's will but also gave the individual a blessing for their task. The second reason resulted from the growth of the Church. The Apostles transferred the gifts they had received to those who were baptised through the laying on of hands. There are numerous biblical descriptions of people receiving the Holy Spirit through this action. But as the Church spread the Apostles and the bishops they chose to follow them could not be in every place that the laying on of hands was needed. And so they instituted the

Holy Chrism, oil which would carry the blessing of the bishops and which could be administered by the presbyters.

The Church baptises and chrismates children because we do not believe that someone can be only partly in the Church: one is either a member or not. To baptise infants but withhold chrismation is a western practice that comes from the idea that we must make a personal commitment before God will unite Himself to us. In fact Christ admonished the disciples for denying children the opportunity to come to Him and we believe that it is unthinkable that God would withhold His grace and Kingdom from any child. There are a number of reasons to take this position even beyond the words of Christ. When someone converted to Judaism it was the tradition for the man's whole household to be received and similarly in the Book of Acts (Chapters 11 and 16) we read of the Apostles adopting this same approach to converts to Christianity. We also read of how John the Baptist was filled with God's Spirit even in his mother's womb and in the Psalms we are told that God knows us from the moment of our conception. The mystery of faith is not limited to rational expressions of belief; the human heart can meet with God regardless of mental development or ability.

There are many Orthodox who do not appreciate the full importance of Holy Chrism and how it acts as one of the bonds that unites us each to the other.

The oil itself is made up of different scented oils; in Constantinople the Ecumenical Patriarch has an official list of ingredients which includes fifty-seven elements. The rite to produce it proceeds over a number of days in Holy Week and when local churches receive the Holy Chrism from their patriarch they are acknowledging his role as successor to the Apostles but also expressing their unity in faith.

At the time of being received into the Church we also make our confession and if this is someone's first time it can often feel a daunting task. But it should never be something we dread; in fact Saint John Chrysostom encourages us to run to confession at every opportunity that our souls may find the joy of its consolation.

Confession

"Just as a man is enlightened by the Holy Spirit when he is baptised by a priest so he who confesses his sins with a repentant heart obtains remission from the priest."
~ Saint Athanasius

Saint John Chrysostom teaches us to think of the Church not as a court of law but as a hospital: not a place of judgement but one of healing. The sacraments are like medicines for the soul and confession is the instrument by which we treat the sickness. It might be better to refer to it as the sacrament of repentance rather than confession since, as we shall see, confession is only one part of what takes place. Let us first consider the authority Christ gave to the Church to administer His forgiveness and then we will reflect on something of the experience and reality of what the sacrament brings.

There are three explicit moments when Christ told His disciples that they were to be responsible for the forgiveness of sins. In the sixteenth chapter, verse 19, of the Gospel of Saint Matthew He says to the Apostles: *whatsoever you shall bind on earth will be bound in Heaven, and whatsoever you loose on earth shall be loosed in Heaven.* Christ goes on to use similar words in verse 18 of the eighteenth chapter too. And in the twentieth chapter, verse 23, of the Gospel of Saint John after blessing the Apostles with the gift of the Holy Spirit, He says: *Whose sins you remit, they are remitted, and whose sins you retain they are retained.*

The first point we should note then is that when the priest pronounces the words of absolution he does not do so in his own authority but in Christ's. It is God Who forgives us but the Church has been given the responsibility and blessing to share this forgiveness with its members. When a member of the Church receives absolution they return to the state of innocence that they were granted as they rose from the waters of baptism. Confession acts to restore us to our blessed state, it is a sign of God's unlimited love and mercy that should fill us with hope. No matter how much we fall away from the promises of our baptism God is able and willing to heal us of the damage our sin has done to us and make us holy once more.

Many of the Church Fathers make a comparison between physical and spiritual sickness. They ask who would not rush to see a doctor and ask for the appropriate medicines if they were afflicted with some disease. It is with this same urgency that we should desire to find healing of soul. Confession brings us a peaceful conscience for which we should all long.

But earlier I mentioned that sometimes we feel daunted at the prospect of admitting our sins before our priest. We are ashamed of our sins and worry that he will think less of us. In fact part of our healing is the growth of our knowledge of ourselves and this requires a level of humility that can grow when we confess our sins. But we must never imagine that our priest ever thinks badly of us for what we are confessing: in fact the opposite is true. A good father confessor will only grow in love for us at the depth and honesty of our confession as he recognises the great faith that prompted us to bare our soul. But we do not do this just to anyone. Saint Basil the Great warns us not to reveal our sickness just to anyone, it does not benefit us to show our physical wounds to someone that is not equipped to help us and neither should we reveal our sins to those who cannot bring us release.

But we must not see confession as some mechanistic system that guarantees us forgiveness. God knows our sins in greater depth than our own memories can recall and it is important for us not to hide anything out of shame. But also confession requires that we commit ourselves to struggle against our sins. The opportunity to talk in depth with our priest about our inner state can itself be of great value and provides an opportunity to reflect on how we are living and how we can fight more courageously against sin in the future. Confession cleanses us but it does not protect us from sinning again. We must not only speak the words but feel a genuine sense of remorse over what we have done. The Fathers describe a need for us to weep over our sins, to genuinely purge ourselves of evil.

Earlier I mentioned that confession is really only one part of the sacrament, we also need contrition and affliction. Confession is speaking aloud about our sins and contrition is the grief we feel knowing that we have offended God. It is the response of love for the One Who loves us completely. But we must also be afflicted by the damage we have done to ourselves and recognise the danger we have placed ourselves in by rejecting the Kingdom of God by sinning. When we see this truth we often experience a great longing for repentance and so escape the sin and grief which torments us.

A genuine desire for repentance is essential for a healing confession and there are a number of things we can do to help ourselves achieve it. The first step is to genuinely believe with all our heart that God is willing to forgive us and that He has entrusted the Church with this authority. Next we should remind ourselves of the great debt we owe to God and how we have returned His love with our sin. Time and again Christ taught that if we wish to be forgiven we must forgive others. In confession we must have a true desire to forgive those who have wronged us, and let go of both the serious and petty hurts which we carry in our hearts. It is also necessary to acknowledge how we have hurt others and seek their forgiveness as we admit our wrongs.

Saint John of Damascus teaches us that repentance can be summed up as returning from the devil to God. We should know that demons work to attract us away from God, that our sins are like serpents nipping at our hearts, pulling us into the devil's embrace. Repentance is a sword that cuts off the heads of these serpents; we must not let the demons use our pride to persuade us to drop this mighty weapon. We stand in the heat of battle whether we choose to fight or not, and confession is a gift from the One Who has already won the war and now offers us a taste of His victory.

The Eucharist

"After partaking of the Eucharist, our bodies are no longer corruptible, having the hope of eternal

resurrection."
~ Saint Irenaeus

The Church's understanding of Holy Communion is unchanged in two thousand years. However, there have in more recent centuries arisen different heresies which must be distinguished from the truth. We will first establish that from the very beginning the Church believed that the bread and wine became the Body and Blood of Christ, and that this was universally accepted before Roman legalism created a misunderstanding which was then rejected by Protestants who then created their own false teachings. We shall look at how these teachings differ from the doctrine of the Church and then reflect on the value and purpose of receiving Holy Communion. Finally we will look at the issue of how often we should receive Holy Communion and how different attitudes have developed.

Before the Great Schism all Christians believed that they received the actual Body and Blood of Christ but for a thousand years the Church recognised that a great mystery was at work that could not be defined or dissected with rational explanations. As the West later embraced what was proudly called the Age of Reason in the eleventh and twelfth centuries, Latin scholastic thinking felt compelled to provide a complete explanation of what was taking place in the *mass*. The resulting doctrine was called *transubstantiation* which had at its foundation a distorted view of Christ's Ascension which resulted in a materialistic explanation of the Eucharist. Being rationalists themselves, the Protestant thinkers do not accept Rome's teaching and the majority claim that in the Eucharist we receive nothing but ordinary bread and wine (with a few variations in wording to make it at least seem a bit special).

The Latin philosophers declared that after His Ascension Christ inhabited a particular space, that His physical body must in some sense remain within the limits of the physical existence of all our human bodies. Therefore the idea behind transubstantiation is that Christ moves His physical presence from one place to another; from the heavenly realm to the earthly bread and wine. But the Church teaches that Christ is not limited to a single place in this way, He transcends all boundaries of location, He has departed from the material world without abandoning it: by His will He is able to be anywhere and everywhere. The fundamental issue is that Latin scholars reduced Christ to an *object* which continues to exist in the cosmos in the same way that all objects exist in the universe. But Christ's resurrection and ascension have transfigured His humanity so that He is no longer limited in this way.

For the Church the bread and wine are not materially transformed by moving Christ's Body from one place to another, but are united to Him in a miraculous manner. This means they no longer exist as independent things of the world but have been joined to Christ in the heavenly realm while still maintaining the physical qualities of earthly objects. Through the bread and wine Christ enters into communion with the created universe and we are invited to enter into communion with Him. He does not abandon His Body that is now glorified within the Godhead but through the descent of the Holy Spirit makes Himself present in them. The bread and wine must retain their outward physical properties in order that we may consume them and so be united with Him.

That the early Church believed in the reality of Christ's Body and Blood in the Eucharist is confirmed in countless writings from the time. First we will remind ourselves of what the New Testament says and then look at writings from the first three hundred years of the Church's existence to reinforce the point that the early Christians took Christ's presence in the Eucharist for granted.

Christ taught us that *he who eats my flesh and drinks my blood abides in me and I in him* (John 6 v56). Here we have a direct teaching from our Lord that we are united with Him through our receiving of Holy Communion. In verse 58 of the same chapter He goes on to promise that *He who eats this bread will live forever.* Our union with Christ is necessary to receive eternal life

In his first letter to the church in Corinth Saint Paul writes:

The cup of blessing which we bless, is it not a participation in the Blood of Christ? The bread which we break, is it not a participation in the Body of Christ? Because there is one bread, we who are many are one body, for we all partake of the one bread.

Here Saint Paul not only teaches the reality of the Eucharist but also calls us to recognise the unity created between us as the Body of Christ through our participation in the Eucharist. In the eleventh chapter (verses 23 to 27) Saint Paul warns that anyone who participates unworthily in the Eucharist is guilty of profaning the sacrament and we are warned that to do so is to bring judgement on ourselves. The notion of unworthiness will be discussed later but first let us acknowledge that if the Protestant idea of the bread and wine being no more than symbols or an act of remembrance, then this warning makes no sense: bread and wine used in this way can result in no such effect.

The early Church writers were clear in their understanding of the Eucharist. Saint Ignatius as a boy had heard the Apostle John preach and as bishop of Antioch he wrote around 90 A.D. in a letter to the Smyrnaeans concerning a group of heretics:

They abstain from prayer and the Eucharist because they do not admit that the Eucharist is the flesh of our Saviour Jesus Christ, the flesh which suffered for our sins and which the Father in His graciousness raised from the dead.

103

Saint Justin Martyr wrote in his first apology around 150 A.D. that *the food consecrated by the Word of prayer which comes from Him, from which our flesh and blood are nourished by transformation, is the flesh and blood of that incarnate Jesus.*

Saint Irenaus of Lyons wrote in 180 A.D.:

For just as the bread which comes from the earth, having received the invocation of God, is no longer ordinary bread, but the Eucharist consisting of two realities, earthly and heavenly, so our bodies, having received the Eucharist, are no longer corruptible, because they have the hope of the resurrection.

A little later in 350 A.D. Saint Ephraim wrote:

Our Lord Jesus took in His hands what in the beginning was only bread, and he blessed it, and signed it, and made it holy in the name of the Father and in the name of the Spirit: and he broke it and in His gracious kindness He distributed it to all His disciples one by one. He called the bread His living Body, and did Himself fill it with Himself and the Spirit.

Saint Athanasius who was present at the First Ecumenical Council in Nicea declares in a sermon of 373 A.D.:

So long as the prayers of supplication and entreaties have not been made, there is only bread and wine. But after the great and wonderful prayers have been completed, then the bread is become the Body, and the wine the Blood, of our Lord Jesus Christ.

Our final example comes from Saint Gregory of Nyssa who very explicitly teaches the Church's faith in 383 A.D.: *The bread is at first common bread, but when the mystery sanctifies it, it is called and actually becomes the Body of Christ.*

There are different attitudes and traditions within Orthodoxy regarding how often we should receive Holy Communion and this is nothing to be concerned about. In fact practice has never been completely static. By the second century there was a move away from the Eucharist being celebrated along with the Agape meal which may reflect the growing Gentile membership of the Church. Many members of the early Church communicated daily (a practice still encouraged later by Saint John Chrysostom) and it was considered such a necessary part of Christian life that the 9th Apostolic Canon was introduced which demanded that anyone who left the Liturgy before receiving Holy Communion should be excommunicated. Compare this with the practice in mid-nineteenth century Russia where it was normal to approach Holy Communion only once a year and only after having made Confession. Let us consider how this difference in approach developed and what should be our practice today.

The warning from Saint Paul that *he that eateth and drinketh unworthily, eateth and drinketh damnation to himself* (1Cor.11 v29) is often the basis for hesitancy about receiving frequently. Feelings of unworthiness are right, we are unworthy and a true understanding of ourselves only reinforces this view. We all sin; none of us is yet perfected. But alongside this we must be aware of God's forgiveness. The fact is, it is our sinfulness that makes it necessary to receive Holy Communion: in the Eucharist we find healing, forgiveness, strength, spiritual nourishment and a defence against Satan. And knowing that we are to receive Holy Communion should encourage us to live more holy lives, we should live in preparedness for the moment when we will be given Christ's Body and Blood. In humility we approach the chalice recognising our unworthiness but placing our hope and trust in God's mercy. Saint John Chrysostom assures us that through Holy Communion God will *completely burn away your sins and will fill your souls with light and sanctification.*

The canons of the Church specify that we must receive Holy Communion at least once every year. But if we allow a long period of time to lapse between receiving we will grow accustomed to the life of sin we can fall into and remembering our sins will be almost impossible if we allow many weeks to go by. It is spiritually unhealthy to go long periods without receiving Holy Communion and we must not allow anything to convince us otherwise.

One reason some people do not receive frequently is because they do not believe they have prepared properly, and sometimes this is because they have a false idea of what is required of them. We must fast from all food and drink from midnight before receiving. If we have failed to fast on the preceding Wednesday and Friday it should have no bearing on our decision. We are not required to fast all of the day before: in fact the sixty fourth canon of the Holy Apostles forbids fasting on Saturdays except on a few important feasts. But for many people the crucial factor is whether they have been to confession. We must be clear that there are different traditions within Orthodoxy concerning this: for some it is considered necessary to always make confession before receiving while other traditions see confession as a periodic act that does not always have to come before Holy Communion. Certainly for priests who receive Holy Communion at every Divine Liturgy the question is not raised as to whether they have always been to confession: and so there is the view that the laity should not be burdened with a demand that is not carried equally by the clergy. However, if someone does not receive Holy Communion regularly then it is more appropriate for them to make their confession first.

The Church does not see Holy Communion as nothing more than a memorial because we believe it is a miraculous event which unites us to the saving death and resurrection of Christ. The

Eucharist transforms us by giving us the new life of Christ. Writers as early as Saint Ignatius recognised the Church as a *Eucharistic Society*, it is what defines our nature and gives us eternal life. Unless we have committed fornication, blasphemy, sodomy, witchcraft etc. then we have an obligation to receive Holy Communion. God offers us His grace, He calls us to receive, but the devil longs for us to find excuses for why we should refuse. And even if we have committed serious offences against God we must rush to our priest and confess and be forgiven. For none of us knows when our soul will be demanded of us.

Ordination

"The priesthood is performed on earth but it possesses the order of heavenly things."
~ Saint John Chrysostom

The hierarchy within the Church was established by Christ and preserved by the Holy Spirit in order to maintain the continuity of the faith and the inner life of the Church. The sacrament of ordination enables priests and bishops to serve in a ministry of grace which maintains the good order of the Church: hence the name Holy Orders. Through the sacrament a man becomes the representative of the people as he stands at the altar. But he also takes on the role of being an icon of Christ to his people while bishops stand as direct successors to the

Apostles. When a priest stands in prayer he brings to God not only his own concerns but those of his whole parish. However, we must be careful how we understand this idea. The priest as icon does not suggest that Christ is not present; the priest's role is not to represent one who is missing, but enable the people to draw closer to the One in their midst.

But there are contemporary Christians who have fallen away from the Church's practice believing ordination to be a later development in the life of the Church. In fact we find ordination through the laying on of hands described in the New Testament. In Acts (6 v2-6) we read of men being selected and then having hands laid upon them. This double-action is always necessary: it is the people who first elect those for ordination but it is God who ordains. This is made very clear at Orthodox ordinations when the people are required to shout *Axios!* (*worthy*) to demonstrate their approval of the candidate. Priesthood does not belong to the one who receives it but is given for the good of the community.

At first the Apostles themselves ordained deacons and presbyters and when we read the accounts in Acts of Saints Paul and Barnabas doing this it is clear that it was more than an empty ritual: it was the means by which God's grace was given in a profound and definite way. We hear of this gift in the letter to Saint Timothy when Saint Paul says: *Do not neglect the gift that is in you, which you received through prophecy and the laying on of hands by the presbytery (1Tim. 4 v14).*

Saint Clement reinforces this double-action when he writes *The election of men for the priesthood is the work of men; but the ordination of them is not the work of men but the work of God.* The priesthood is a sacred action which a man can only receive once in his life. The Church accepts married men for the priesthood but once he is ordained a man may not then become married. An impairment to priesthood is if a man has had a previous marriage or if his wife has been married before. Roman Catholicism demands that its priests be celibate despite the fact that this was once more rejected by the Sixth Ecumenical Council.

The modern role of the priest incorporates many things that the bishop would have originally done: teaching, praying for the sick, celebrating the Eucharist and so on. But as the Church grew it was necessary to give responsibility for some of these actions to priests since the bishop could not attend to everything. Today the priest continues to do everything in the authority of his bishop. When he celebrates the Eucharist he must always have the antimension spread out over the altar or the Eucharist cannot happen (a Eucharist without it would be seen to be something outside the Church). The antimension is a cloth depicting the wounds of Christ and is signed by the bishop. It is the sign that what the community is doing is in accordance with Apostolic tradition and has the bishop's blessing.

It is normal for ordained men to be called Father but this is a term of endearment rather than any formal title and when writing to a priest it is common to address him as *Reverend Father.* If one is writing to an archpriest, protopresbyter or archimandrite it is the custom to address them as *the Very Reverend.* We should note that while all who receive ordination are called to struggle to meet their high calling and responsibility they remain sinful men and these titles should not lead us to create fantasies about the sanctity of our clergy, however decent and worthy particular examples may be. The reality of the sacraments that they celebrate is not affected by their individual sinfulness since it is Christ Who acts through their actions, it is Christ Who heals or forgives or bestows His grace.

The deacons of the Church originally served the people as a kind of assistant to the bishop, performing acts of charity and care for members of the Body. However, over time the deacon's role acquired an important liturgical character and today it is the deacon who leads the litanies in our services amongst other functions.

Before we move on to our next topic we should briefly mention the issue of the ordination of women. There is evidence that deaconesses served in the Church and the practice may have continued for a number of centuries. There is disagreement amongst scholars about their exact role; some see them as having been female deacons while others suggest they may have had different duties. It could be that a male clergyman may have been an inappropriate presence in some circumstances and in female monastic communities there is clearly a practical reason for the priest to be assisted by a woman in this way. The ordination of women to the priesthood is not a pressing issue amongst Orthodox Christians and so the Church has never felt the need to address it in any formal way. It is not a topic I have ever heard raised amongst Orthodox and therefore not something I will pursue here.

Holy Unction

"The bishop prays over the oil asking that the prayers give strength to all who taste it and strength to all who use it."
~ From the Apostolic Tradition

In the Old and New Testaments we find countless examples of oil being associated with grace and the replenishing of life and joy. Just as in the sacrament of Chrismation oil is used in Holy Unction both as a sign of God's presence and the giving of strength and healing. We read in the Gospel of Saint Mark an example of oil used in this way, he says that they *anointed with oil many that were sick and healed them* (Mk 6 v13). We find the instruction to anoint the sick with oil in the Epistle of Saint James (Ch 5 v14) and it is clear that the ritual was to be performed by the presbyters within a liturgical setting.

Amongst Roman Catholics the sacrament is only administered when someone is thought to be dying (a practice introduced in the twelfth century in contradiction to the teaching of Saint James) but in the Church all who are sick or recognise their need for spiritual healing may receive it: in effect this is everyone. On the Wednesday of Holy Week there is an invitation to all Orthodox to receive this anointing as part of the preparation for Pascha.

When we receive this sacrament we are anointed seven times on the head, mouth, hands etc as in our Chrismation. We believe that it gives us every kind of healing and can enable us to repent and strive to draw closer to God. The underlying principle is that it is a further support for us in our Christian lives and not simply as something saved for the time before death. Orthodoxy stresses the importance of the way we live and how we are unable to fulfil our calling as members of the Church without God's grace.

Marriage

"We do not deny that marriage has been sanctified by Christ since the Divine Word says "The two shall become one flesh and one spirit.""
~ Saint Ambrose

While there are other Christian organisations that claim to celebrate these sacraments when it comes to the understanding of marriage we also have to recognise the influence of secular groups and even social trends. To do this we will again look to the biblical evidence in Genesis and what Jesus revealed before considering how the early Church viewed marriage. Finally we will look at what it means for us to see marriage as a sacrament and how this should impact on our lives.

In Genesis we read of how God created all things. It is interesting to note that the birds, fish and other animals are simply named by their species or type whereas man is created and named as male and female. The Church recognises this as revealing something fundamental to our nature, that men and women are both different and complimentary. This finds a fuller expression when God declares that *It is not good for man to be alone.* We are created to exist in community, in relationship with one another. Our sexual identity is there at the beginning of time, it is not a consequence of the fall or something society has created.

When Jesus was asked by the Pharisees about the legitimacy of divorce their concern was really about the legality of it under the Law, but Jesus refers back to Genesis in His answer and identifies the ontological reality of our gender. The Bible makes it clear to us that God did not intend for man to exist alone but specifically, as Jesus quotes: *From the beginning God made them male and female.* The nature of the relationship God intended us to exist within was between a man and wife.

The early Church placed the celebration of marriage firmly within the context of the Eucharist. The act of bringing people together in marriage was always performed alongside Holy Communion because the Christian life they would be sharing was always seen to be with and in Christ. Today this is reflected in the marriage service by many things being done three times, the actions with the rings, the crowns and so on, reminding us that with the couple the Person of Christ is present.

This leads us to the belief that marriage is a sacrament. In their union the two people become a reflection of God's Kingdom, a small church, as Saint John Chrysostom writes, *Marriage is a mystical icon of the Church.* And no church can exist without Christ at its centre. This is a unique understanding of marriage that is different to a sociological, anthropological or legal concept. While the society around us reduces marriage to a legal contract we maintain that it is a source of grace which should draw us closer to Christ. Whatever national laws we live under we should never allow them to deny this sacramental nature of marriage. It must always be for us a sign of how God is restoring us and the whole cosmos back to communion with Himself. Therefore we should see marriage as a means of discovering the living reality of God's Kingdom. By becoming one flesh the man and woman are an expression of Christ's own unity with His Church, we witness to the love of God's Kingdom through our love for one another. Here we speak of God's love which is beyond sentiment, but is an act of will, it requires that we struggle to maintain it, that we be willing to sacrifice ourselves for it: it is ultimately a form of asceticism.

The marriage service reflects these ideas in its structure and prayers. Orthodox weddings have two parts: the Betrothal and the Crowning. The Betrothal involves the exchange of rings but does not require the couple to make vows which really serve a kind of legal function. It is in the Crowning that the Church's faith becomes more apparent as we celebrate the couple becoming king and queen of the little kingdom that they have become but also that they now wear martyrs' crowns. While this links to the idea of asceticism we must also understand the meaning of *martyr* as witness: every marriage becomes a witness to the salvation of God's Kingdom.

Of course we must not romanticise marriage and for many the experience may seem to be less the Kingdom of God and more an arena of trials. But the two are not incompatible, when marriage is a place of testing it is then that we may demonstrate our true love of God. It is when we face the fallen reality of ourselves and our spouse that we must choose to forgive, to be patient, to continue to love even when the passions tempt us to abandon our commitments. It is when we choose to be obedient to God and accept the other in all their spiritual nakedness that we are given the grace to truly love and build God's Kingdom.

While many doctrines of the Church have been developed and explored to astounding depth it is fair to say that marriage has not received the same level of focus. There is a simple reason for this: many of the great theological writings were produced to defend the Church's faith from heresies. Until our modern age marriage has not needed the same degree of explanation because few have attacked it or challenged traditional thinking. Today in the West we have a plethora of theories competing for acceptance and it may be that the Church will have to present more defined theological expressions of the truth. The main differences between the Church and secular society concern sexuality and its relation to marriage. Put simply the Church teaches that marriage can only be the union of two people, male and female. In the United Kingdom the existence of Civil Partnerships has led to a legalistic view of marriage where the couple are simply entering a legal relationship and are bound by particular laws. As a result they have no objection to two people of the same gender entering this legal contract. The Church teaches that there is no such thing as a homosexual marriage since it is an ontological impossibility. Male and female are not interchangeable realities and the legal dimensions of marriage do not determine what a marriage is, they are only a part of it.

Confusion about human sexuality has left some people uncertain about how they should think about sexuality in general. Many moralistic Christian groups have approached the whole topic of sexuality from the wrong direction: instead of it being at the heart of who we are and intended to be by God they see it as something that must be coped with or somehow excused. This is because they have a view of sexuality that is debased and associated with sinful passions. Much of this has come from the writings of Augustine who saw sexuality in terms of our fallen nature and not as a blessing. Certainly after the fall we have become predisposed to treating sex as we do so many other things, that is for personal satisfaction or individual fulfilment. But the Church teaches that through our knowledge of the other in sexual union we are able to find a deeper awareness of ourselves and God. When we recognise our beloved as an icon in the image of God we are able to understand our sexuality not as a purely physical or material reality but as a spiritual one.

These themes are reflected in the idea of a marriage being consummated when a couple have sex. Such a notion reduces the union to a legal form of possession (almost always of the woman by the man). But this also reflects a materialistic view of sexuality and union. The true consummation of a marriage requires the giving not just of the body but also the mind and spirit to the other. Even if a couple have shared their wedding bed we can argue that if either of them withhold the deepest parts of themselves then they have rejected this true consummation.

The Orthodox Church recognises that despite our efforts we all continue to sin. Therefore it should not be surprising that sometimes marriages fail. Although we believe that we must enter marriage with the intention of remaining married until one of us dies, we do accept that there are occasions when divorce is permissible. The Church also understands that when a marriage ends a second or even third marriage may be possible (but never more). In such circumstances a second marriage involves a penitential tone which reflects the failure of what has gone before but enables the couple to participate fully in the life of the Church.

Marriage is a mystery which can never be fully understood until we enter and experience it. There are universal aspects to marriage but the union of two individuals is a unique and specific reality that is like a tiny cosmos unto itself. The couple must enter a kind of spiritual desert where they remove themselves from the temptations of the world around them to discover a deeper reality. Just as God's creation of the universe is an act of love so we are given a share in His creativity through our love for one another. Our union, our love and our sexuality take on a holy nature because through them we participate with God in the creation of other human beings. And in our marriages we teach our children to glimpse God's Kingdom as we attempt to model it in our lives. In marriage we assume responsibility for one another's salvation, and with the gift of God's grace we manifest in our union something of the union of the Holy Trinity.

What Do The Parts of The Divine Liturgy Mean?

"We do not consume the Eucharistic bread as if it were ordinary food and drink, for we have been taught that as Jesus our Saviour became a man of flesh and blood by the power of the Word of God, so also the food that our flesh and blood assimilates for its nourishment becomes the Flesh and Blood of the incarnate Jesus by the power of His own words contained in the prayer of thanksgiving."

~ Saint Justin Martyr

The sacrifice Christ made of Himself is an unrepeatable act that makes possible our resurrection and salvation: all will be resurrected and some will be saved. In the Divine Liturgy this sacrifice is made real in our lives, as the theologians say it is *actualised*, it becomes a living reality for us through the Eucharist. The Eucharist can never be reduced to a symbolic memorial; it is a miraculous event, a mystery in which all members of the Church must participate to experience Christ's resurrected life within them. The words and actions become very familiar to us but their meaning is not always fully understood. Father Thomas Hopko has a series of podcasts available on Ancient Faith Radio which explain the Liturgy in precise detail and which last many hours. I will not attempt to go into anywhere near as much detail here but instead identify some of the reasons for our liturgical actions so that we can understand a little more of what it is we are doing.

One of the first differences we see in an Orthodox church compared with other places of worship is the absence of pews (unless the building previously belonged to a different tradition and they have been retained). This reflects the practice of the early Church and historians suggest that congregations didn't start taking to their seats until the seventeenth century in the West and much later in the East. An absence of pews means worshippers are free to move around more easily in order to light candles or venerate icons. There is also an element of asceticism in standing for the whole service and many younger converts to Orthodoxy are often surprised at how comfortable older Orthodox people seem to be standing for long periods. As our legs and back begin to complain we have a small opportunity to exert our will over the body. Standing in worship also creates a sense of participation rather than being a seated audience to what is happening, standing also creates a sense of expectation that something important is happening. The lack of regimentation that rows of pews can suggest also enhances the sense of gathering, that the congregation forms a single group not separated by furniture. One point to make about the freedom to move around however, is that there are key moments when it is not appropriate to approach the iconostasis to light a candle: these are during the Epistle and Gospel readings, while the Little and Great Entrances are taking place, during the Anaphora (when the bread and wine is being consecrated on the altar) and when the priest is delivering his sermon.

The altar is placed at the east end of the church to remind us of our own journey east, which symbolises the Kingdom of God. We also read in the Book of Revelation that Christ's return will be from the east and so we worship looking in anticipation for His coming. The processions which bring first the Gospel Book and then the offerings of bread and wine also move eastwards, again reminding us of how geographical and physical space is transformed in faith into a spiritual map guiding us towards Christ.

The Liturgy begins with the priest censing the church: he begins by censing the altar and the gifts, the iconostasis and then the congregation. This is an act of purification, a making ready of the place and people for what is about to happen. Incense is also a sign of the prayers which ascend to the throne of God and its use has its roots in the Old Testament. There is another aspect to our use of incense which is the involvement of all our senses in worship. The visual beauty of the icons, the sober and yet joyful singing, the struggle to stand when the body tires, and the sweet smelling smoke of the incense prevent us from imagining that worship is just an intellectual or even inner activity. The involvement of our senses reminds us that we are a union of body and soul and that our salvation requires our whole self to participate. One further reason for burning incense is to communicate the mystery of worship and of God's presence. Both in the Old Testament, such as when Moses ascended the mountain to meet with God, and in the New when the voice of the Father was heard at Christ's Transfiguration, clouds have always represented the presence of God. As our churches fill with the swirling clouds of incense we are reminded that it is the same God now present with us.

The deacon or priest will then lead the congregation in the *Litany of Peace*. It is important to remember that as the priest identifies specific things and people for us to pray for, it is the response of the congregation with *Lord have mercy* which is the actual prayer. Therefore all of us should sing this response in church and not just the choir because it is our collective prayer as a gathered people which is being offered to God.

Much of what is sung in the Divine Liturgy is based on words from the Bible. The Liturgy is an important means of both declaring and teaching the Church's faith. At the beginning of the Liturgy *Antiphons* are sung which are hymns based on the Psalms. They consist of verses sung by the choir with responses sung by the whole congregation. The pattern is that the first Antiphon refers to the

Theotokos, the second to Christ and the third to the feast of that particular Sunday. However, over time the practice in some churches has been to reduce the singing to one Antiphon.

The procession of the Gospel Book is called the Little Entrance and the later procession of the offerings is the Great Entrance. Although there is clearly a liturgical reason for this action, both in terms of direction and in identifying the importance of the objects, there is also a historical reason. During the time of Roman persecution the Church would often have its Gospel Book and sacred vessels stolen. The Romans would often make a great show of destroying the Church's holy objects and so they would be hidden away between services to keep them safe. When the church gathered for worship these things would be brought into the congregation with great honour as signs of God's saving grace, and as the pattern of the Liturgy became established (within seventy years of the Church's existence) these liturgical processions were a fixed part of the service. The candles carried by the servers remind us that Christ is the Light of the world, and that in the gospels we find the grace and light which enlightens our being.

Then follows the *Trisagion Hymn* (Trisagion means "Thrice Holy") which is when we join our voices with the singing of the angels who sing *Holy, Holy, Holy* (Isaiah 6 v3). This threefold singing of *holy* also reminds us that we worship the Holy Trinity and that we worship all three Holy

Persons, Father, Son and Holy Spirit. As we sing this hymn we make the sign of the cross and bow in acknowledgement of God Who is the source of all being, the Maker of all things and the Source of life. The hymn is ancient in origin and is known to have been sung by those gathered at the Council of Ephesus in 431 A.D..

The biblical flavour of our worship is tasted once more when we prepare to hear the Epistle reading. The *Prokimenon* is made up of verses from the Psalms and consists of the choir singing verses followed by responses which the congregation should sing. The particular verses have been chosen to reflect the theme of the Sunday and it is believed that in the early Church the whole Psalm would have been sung: the Psalms are the original hymns of our worship.

Once the Epistle is read we sing Alleluia and more verses from Psalms before the priest censes the Gospel Book. During this censing he does not cense the whole altar area as it is specifically the book that is now our focus. The people are censed so that they may prepare themselves to receive the Gospel message and everyone now stands in recognition of the importance of what is being read (it is the custom for people to sit during the Epistle reading). All four gospels are read through different parts of the year, for example the Gospel of Saint John is read from Pascha night to the feast of Pentecost. In some churches the sermon follows the Gospel so that the teaching is linked to the reading but in other traditions the sermon comes at the very end of the service.

In preparation for the Great Entrance with the holy vessels the Antimension is now unfolded on the altar. A dismissal of the catechumens is sung by the priest which would have marked the point in the early Church when those who had not yet been baptised were expected to leave. While we do not expect the unbaptised to depart we retain these words as a reminder to those preparing for baptism and chrismation that they are yet to enter fully into the Eucharistic community. The priest then bows to the people asking for their forgiveness. Around his shoulders he ties the *aer* which is the larger veil that is placed over the chalice and discos once they are on the altar.

After further prayers we have the Great Entrance which marks the beginning of the second part of the service, the Eucharist. The priest says *The doors, the doors* because in the past this important stage of the service needed to be protected from potential disruption by pagan persecutors and we are reminded by their recital that we do not know when such defence of our mysteries will once again be required.

The saying or singing of the Creed is an important declaration of our shared faith and all the people present should participate. During the Creed the priest waves the aer in the air over the chalice and discos which can easily be misunderstood as it may look to outsiders as though something magical is being done. In fact there are practical, historical reasons for this action but it also conveys something that we believe. Across many parts of the world, from Rome to China and Egypt large ritual fans were used in royal courts to keep the dignitaries free from insects but also as a way of honouring them. These fans were made from feathers and deacons would wave them over the vessels as a reminder of the wings of the angels who invisibly surround the altar during the Eucharist. The aer serves a similar symbolic role as that performed by the curtain at the Royal doors in that when the curtain is drawn back it represents the stone pushed away from the tomb but while the aer covers the vessels it conveys the mystery of hidden things. Like the wings of the angels we are also reminded of the wings of the dove representing the Holy Spirit and as the aer is waved over the vessels we think of the Third Person of the Holy Trinity descending on us and on the gifts offered to transform them and us through His miraculous power. Other writers have suggested that the shaking of the aer in the air is also an indication of the trembling that should be experienced within us as we contemplate the enormity of what is taking place before and in us.

We then begin the Eucharistic Prayer with the priest facing east as he leads the people as one of them. Although the priest and people say the words we believe that it is the Holy Spirit Who transforms the bread and wine into the Body and Blood of

Christ. We say the Lord's Prayer together acknowledging that God provides us with our daily bread which is the meeting of our physical needs but also of our spiritual needs in the Eucharist. As we have said previously, through receiving Holy Communion Christ becomes part of us both spiritually and physically. We normally only use one loaf for the Liturgy to express our unity as God's people. It is the custom in the Church to always receive both the Body and Blood and so they are placed together in the chalice from which the priest communicates us with a spoon. Our physical senses will see and taste bread and wine but the heart of the believer will perceive the power and grace of God: we use the term mystery partly to express the fact that our human logic can not grasp the reality that is taking place.

At the end of the service bread that has been blessed but not consecrated is shared out amongst the people. Known as *Antidoron* this bread is part of the ancient *Agape* meal which Christians shared alongside the Eucharist and which has been retained to remind us that as the Body of Christ we share both the heavenly and earthly gifts of God. In some traditions this bread is only given to those who are members of the Church but in the majority of local churches visitors and non-Orthodox are invited to share in it too. I recall the first Divine Liturgy I attended as an Anglican in 1988 when a monk shared his bread with me and the powerful impression of welcome it made on me. While we must guard access to the Eucharist from the heterodox it is a loving and generous act to share the *Antidoron* with them to make clear our feelings about them showing interest in the Church.

This has been a very brief explanation of some of the things we do in the Divine Liturgy and there are many good resources available to those who wish to know more. The important message to take away from this chapter is that the elements of the service are filled with meaning, and the more we learn the deeper we may be drawn into what is taking place. However, I would encourage people to be careful about how far we try to interpret everything that is being done and how much we apply meaning to every individual action. My reason for saying this is twofold: first we must not reduce the meaning or action of the whole to any one part of the Liturgy. While there is a moment where we invite the Holy Spirit to descend on us and the gifts, we should see the whole Liturgy as part of this process and not fall into a kind of reductionism. Second I would argue that if we analyse every component of the Liturgy we are in danger of losing the sense of mystery that is so important in our experience of worship. In the Liturgy we have a foretaste of the Messianic Banquet, we step beyond the limits of time and space and beyond the limits of our own sinfulness. We experience a miracle far greater than the parting of a sea or turning water into wine: in His love for us Christ transforms that which was grown in the fields and harvested by human hands into His very own Body and Blood. The history, the readings, the symbolic actions, everything we do in the Liturgy is given to us that we may enter this reality.

The Design of Church Buildings

*"The entire sanctuary and spaces around the altar
are filled with the heavenly powers who come to
honour Him Who is present."*
~ Saint John Chrysostom

The design of our churches is nothing less than
an architectural expression of the setting of the
Divine Liturgy. Just as the Eucharist is full of
divine mystery so the design of our churches is
intended to reflect our understanding of the cosmos
and the way God saves us. The ascetic and
liturgical experience of being part of the Church is
made physical in the stone, wood and paint. As
Saint Symeon of Thessalonica tells us:

*Once it is consecrated by a bishop with mystic
prayers and anointed with the holy*
*myrrh it becomes entirely the dwelling place of
God: it contains supernatural grace.*

Our churches lead us deeper into the presence and
love of God through the beauty and organisation of
the space and we should understand that nothing
there is mere decoration or embellishment:
everything is drawn into the liturgical event of the
Eucharist. Just as we recognise that our salvation
concerns our spirit and physical existence so our
churches are part of the sanctification of the
material world.

The intention here is to help us recognise how this is accomplished. Though some historical details will be provided the intention is not to leave you reflecting on historical developments as you stand in church but to make the spiritual meaning clearer. The fact is the early Church used their homes or converted houses for worship until Emperor Constantine (The Great) lifted the ban on Christianity in 313 A.D. and so enabling purpose-built churches to appear. There is a substantial degree of variation in church design from culture to culture but certain characteristics are common to most and these will be our focus.

Before entering the church one feature that immediately sets Orthodox churches apart from other Christian places of worship is the dome. The most famous of these is to be found in the Church of Divine Wisdom (Hagia Sophia) in Constantinople which stood for many centuries as the largest church in the world. It was completed in 537 A.D. and took only six years to complete but what is more remarkable about it is the power of its effect on worshippers. Beneath the dome around its base are forty windows which give the impression that the dome is almost floating in the air: it was described at the time of its building as a *mystical geometry*. In the Church of Divine Wisdom worshippers were left with the sense of the heavens above them. This is precisely the purpose of the dome, unlike the typical roofs of western churches the dome identifies with the celestial dome of

Heaven. The domes of many churches are painted in symbolic colours: green is a symbol of the Holy Trinity; blue domes remind us of the Theotokos and in Russia golden domes are like giant candles symbolising Christ Himself.

Above Russian churches we find the familiar onion-domes which came into existence in the thirteenth century, and which many scholars believe have a pragmatic origin since they make it harder for the heavy snow of Russian winters to accumulate. As well as the colours the number of domes is also significant. The onion domes normally appear in odd numbers: one represents Christ; three symbolises the Holy Trinity; five point to Christ and the Evangelists; seven domes symbolise the seven gifts of the Holy Spirit and so on right up to thirty-three representing Christ's years on earth.

The way the space inside churches is ordered is similarly significant. Despite the cultural and historic variations the most common design has three areas: the narthex, the nave and the sanctuary. These areas create a sense of movement from west to east which is symbolic of our movement from darkness to light, from isolation to union with God and one another. Another way of understanding the orientation to the east is to think of the sunrise as a kind of natural icon of the resurrection in the way the sun rises at the beginning of each new day. A further interpretation is to think of east as symbolising Eden which was the paradise for which we were created. As we move from west to east we recall our ancestors Adam and Eve and the unrestricted communion they had with God before they turned away from Him: at Communion we believe we are being drawn closer to Him. And finally we recall Christ as the *Sun of Righteousness* and look to the rising sun as a sign of the eternal light of Christ Who illuminates His saints.

First we move through the narthex which was traditionally the entrance into the sacred space. In the early centuries of the Church this was where those preparing for baptism would stand during services and where those who had been sanctioned for their behaviour would gather until they were able to receive Holy Communion once more. It was also the place where the poor and needy would wait in order to receive charity from those entering the church. Much of this practice has now passed into history and today those not able to receive Holy Communion are able to freely mix with the rest of the congregation and what was once properly the narthex is now usually used as a place to purchase candles or simply as an entrance.

We then move further into the church into the area where the congregation stands during the services: the nave. The name comes from the Latin for ship, *navis*, which suggests the idea of the occupants being carried heavenward while the storms of life rage around us.

Finally at the east end of the church is the sanctuary, which is the space around the altar beyond the iconostasis. This holy area is reserved for clergy and those assisting them in the services and it is where the altar stands but also where holy vessels, vestments and books are kept and where the bread and wine is prepared before the Divine Liturgy.

The arrangement of these areas can be in a number of forms: many modern Orthodox churches have the interior space arranged as a cross with the outer structure of walls shrouding the whole in a square. Other churches may simply be built in the shape of a cross, called cruciform churches, while others are called basilica churches have a long aisled nave with an apse at one end.

Whichever design is used the essential purpose is to enable the meeting of Heaven and earth: unlike western designs which appear to point heavenward with great towers, Orthodox churches make Heaven known here on earth. As Saint Simeon the New Theologian writes: *The vestibule corresponds to earth, the nave to Heaven and the holy altar to what is above Heaven.* This is why so much of the interior of our churches is curved, or arched, rather than sharp and pointed, and why the icons and wall paintings are within reach and able to be kissed; we are assured that Heaven is within our reach, that God and His salvation, the angels, the saints and all that is hoped for are invisibly close to us, even within us. Just as Christ miraculously united our mortal humanity with His divinity through the incarnation, so our churches raise the earth to

Heaven from where the Holy Spirit once more descends.

Within the church one of the most visually striking and beautiful features is the iconostasis. We shall consider icons in more detail in the next chapter and so for now our focus will be the iconostasis itself. First it is important to remember that it does not separate the nave from the sanctuary but symbolises the connection of the two. The iconostasis represents the border between Heaven and earth but it also signifies, through the images it bears, the union of the two realms achieved through the incarnation of Christ. All separation has been banished and as we stand in worship before the iconostasis we are called to experience the reconciliation of God and man.

Let us first think about how we came to have the iconostasis as we do and then we will focus on its design and function. What we have today is the result of gradual change, an evolution of design. It probably first developed from the Byzantine *templon* in the fifth or sixth century (*templon* coming from *temple* and meaning a kind of chancel screen). One of the earliest descriptions of a screen with icons comes from an English source, the Venerable Bede, who in the seventh century described a rood screen adorned with holy images. Most English screens at this time were not solid and so the description is not of the norm (and probably would not have prompted its description if it had have been). We do know that by the fourteenth century the iconostasis as we would recognise it had taken shape with icons fixed between columns and panels or curtains filling the gaps to form a solid screen. It is important to remember that the height of an iconostasis is not a matter of dogma and there is considerable variation between local churches. In Russia for example it has developed into a structure of five tiers containing different groups of icons but this is more complex than in most traditions.

In its most basic form the iconostasis consists of a horizontal beam beneath which are three sets of doors: the deacon's doors to the North and South and the Royal Doors in the middle of the structure. The deacon's doors normally remain closed other than when someone passes through them but the opening and closing of the Royal Doors has great significance during the services. They have been likened to the gates of paradise and their opening and closing is full of symbolism that heightens our awareness of the themes in our worship but also adds to the liturgical drama. As a symbol of our entrance to the Kingdom of God the Royal Doors may be likened to the entrance to the Holy of Holies in the Jerusalem Temple, and so their opening reminds us of the moment when the curtain was torn open during the crucifixion signifying the lifting of the barrier between man and God. The closing of the curtains also reminds us that our access to God is not to be taken lightly or for granted, we have no right to such access but receive it as a gift though we are unworthy of it. Some writers have identified the shutting of the curtains at the beginning of Great Lent as representing the shutting of paradise to Adam and Eve and the priest then is seen in the role of standing before the gates asking for God's forgiveness.

They are called the Royal Doors because it is the King of Glory, the King of Kings Who passes through them at the Eucharist. Before this of course the bread and wine are carried into the sanctuary through the Royal Doors as the earth's offering and it is these simple things that are transformed and given to us for salvation. Again this reinforces the link between Heaven and earth and reminds us of the reality of our own transformation through God's grace. Similarly the priest carries the Gospel Book through the doors as a sign of the Word of God descending from Heaven to the hearts of the faithful. During Bright Week the Royal Doors remain open as a joyous sign of the mystery of Pascha and worshippers have a clear view of all that occurs at the altar and within the rest of the sanctuary.

The particular icons placed on the different parts of the iconostasis are also important. To either side of the Royal Doors Christ and the Theotokos are always found because they are our means to entering paradise: Christ our King and God and the Theotokos, the one through whom God took flesh for our salvation. On the deacon's doors are icons of angels who minister at the Eucharist with the priest or else saints who were deacons (such as Saint Stephen) and served at the altar while on earth. Above the Royal Doors is usually an icon of the last Supper reminding us of the first Holy Communion and at which the institution of the Eucharist occurred. It is normal to find above or beside this icons of the twelve major feasts of the liturgical year. On the Royal Doors themselves is the icon of the Annunciation reminding us that the Theotokos is herself a kind of door through which Christ entered the physical universe and so is also a type of door through which we in turn enter Heaven.

Though members of the laity should never pass through the Royal Doors when they open, even when we move forwards to receive Holy Communion, we should remember that here we are receiving Christ Who has come from paradise to save us and Who once more gives His Body and Blood to us on earth so that we may enter the eternal gates of Heaven. In one sense the iconostasis represents the fullness of the arguments that the Church developed against those who attacked the use of icons in general, reminding us that in our worship we have stepped from one world to another because God first passed between these worlds. Let us now turn our attention to the icons themselves both in church and in our homes and reflect on why they are so important in Orthodox worship and belief.

The Importance of Icons

"The icon is a song of triumph and a revelation. It is an enduring monument to the victory of the saints."
~ Saint John of Damascus

While there was a decorative aspect to the art of the early Church its main purpose was to teach the faith and elevate the minds of worshippers. Often congregations which may have been illiterate could be taught the basics of the faith through images but the beauty and symbolism was first intended to help Christians become aware of the presence of God amongst them and the great mystery that they were being drawn into. The use of icons is an apostolic practice and we believe that the first icons created of Christ and the Theotokos were completed by Saint Luke.

The word *icon* simply means *image* in Greek and this is a concept that is at the heart of Orthodox belief. Man was created in the image of God and though our sin has corrupted the universe we do not believe that God's image has been utterly destroyed. Through His incarnation Christ came to restore the fullness of that image and through His physical resurrection and ascension has reconciled the human and the divine in every way; including our physical being. Matter itself in Christ's humanity was taken up to God so that the created cosmos is capable of being drawn up into worship of God. We read in Genesis that God created the world and pronounced it *good* and through Christ all things are being restored to that goodness. Therefore it is our belief that spirit and matter should be united in worship of God and icons are one important part of this.

Christians do not worship icons, we do not worship the wood and paint but Christ whose image is presented to us in the icon and we similarly venerate the saints. In periods of history where the Church came into contact with pagans who did worship statues and other idols it was important to make Christian practice clearly distinct. Around 730 A.D. Emperor Leo III banned the use of icons because of his heretical understanding of Christ's incarnation. For over a hundred years iconoclasts (those who rejected icons) destroyed holy images and many people lost their lives in the conflict. This was the reason for the calling of the Seventh Ecumenical Council at which icons were not only declared acceptable in worship but were deemed a necessary component of Christian worship.

Holy saints such as John Damascene were able to make clear the distinction between an image and its prototype. Saint John explained that the two were different, distinct entities which should not be confused because of the likeness they share. Saint

John taught that when Christians venerate the image portrayed in paint and wood it is not the physical substance that is being venerated but the one who is portrayed, the prototype. When the iconoclasts were forced to defend their position the root of their mistake was revealed as believing that God could not be represented. This was a denial of the incarnation and of the belief that Christ is truly God Who came to earth as a man. The Church maintained that since Christ had a physical form which could be seen with physical eyes then it was not only possible to convey His likeness in an image but that to do so was a proclamation of His incarnation. The heresy did not entirely go away however, the Protestants returned to these false ideas at the Reformation and sacred images were smashed once more. Today we always kiss an icon before receiving Holy Communion as a way of demonstrating that we are truly orthodox but also as a sign of the victory of Orthodoxy over heresy. On the first Sunday of Great Lent called the Sunday of Orthodoxy we carry icons in procession to celebrate that God has protected the Church from the iconoclasts.

When we first look at icons we immediately see that they have a style and form which is different to other types of art. Those who write icons (we use the word *write* instead of paint to make clear the theological nature of an icon) do not attempt to capture the appearance of someone as they are in this world but as they live in Heaven. It is not simple flesh and blood which is portrayed but something of the mystery of the resurrected body which will be different to the one we have now. The image is of a form of existence that is more real than the one we see with natural eyes, but not one born out of imagination; it is a reality revealed by God. This is why iconographers must spend time fasting and praying before producing an icon, it is the result of the Church's experience of this other reality that is being communicated.

This is also why the images themselves are never painted to convey a sentimental perspective. It is not human emotion that is our concern, or the physical beauty of a person, but the heights of virtue which they reached: icons convey God's love in His saints, through their suffering, their patience, their humility and so on. An icon reveals to us spiritual values and in the faces of the saints we see dignity and a certain gravity. Icons never portray people with open mouths or laughter or even with superficial smiles; instead they present to us stillness. Icons invite us to step out of the noise and busyness of our world so that our hearts may be freed of earthly cares and filled with God's grace. Similarly icons may appear to have a different sense of perspective to photographic images and they never include shadows or the sun in order to show that for those in Heaven all light comes from God.

As well as the particular approach to the forms of those portrayed, the colours used in icons also have symbolic meaning. First, blue is used as a symbol of Heaven and the mysteries of God. Red conveys life because of its association with blood but also communicates vitality and beauty. In Orthodox icons the Theotokos is normally robed in red rather than the western images of her which dress her in blue. White is used to symbolise purity and innocence and can also express the sense of the divine world. Green is associated with youth and fertility and gold communicates the glory of God and life in His heavenly Kingdom.

When I first visited Mount Athos I quickly discovered that the practice of venerating icons with repeated bows was not the way the monks did things. The monastic approach was far simpler and less time consuming but in our parishes we have different traditions. Normally we make the sign of the cross and then a metanoia and do this twice before kissing the icon followed by a third sign of the cross and final metanoia. In some traditions this is reserved for icons of Christ and the Theotokos and all other saints are venerated after a simple sign of the cross. In Lent we replace metanoias with prostrations. When we venerate icons we must never kiss the face of Christ or the saint as this demonstrates over-familiarity and disrespect; we kiss the hands or feet just as we would not kiss a bishop on the cheek but instead reverently kiss his hand.

Icons are not intended only to be used in church but all Orthodox Christians should have icons in their home. We do this for many reasons, the first being to remind ourselves of God's presence with us in our homes. Each family should consider itself as being a small church and the presence of icons reminds us to live as such. It is important to choose a part of the home to dedicate to prayer, often called an icon wall or corner. It helps us to have a specific place for prayer in our homes and it serves to remind us to say our prayers. Although we should try to live as Christians in every part of our home, it is good to create a sacred space which can help us to adopt a prayerful state when we go to it. Some homes have huge collections of icons while others exhibit just one or two: the number isn't important. We should try to have an icon of Christ and the Theotokos and many people find it useful to have icons of their patron saints; beyond this is simply a matter of personal choice.

In some traditions the icon corner is referred to as the *home altar* which reinforces the sense of the family as a church but must not be confused with an actual altar where the Eucharist is celebrated. Many Orthodox keep prayer books, bottles of holy water, oil and relics where they pray in the home and it is certainly useful to have holy objects such as these near us when we pray. A good practice is to light candles before the icons when we pray just as we do when we go to church. The smell and light can help us to enter into a prayerful state and incense is also useful. On Mount Athos they encourage people to keep candle flames small and

146

constant rather than large flickering ones because they can act as a reminder of sobriety and humility. But any type of candle that is used is better than none at all.

There is so much more to say concerning the theology and use of icons but the aim here has really been to remind us of the importance of icons and help us to value them more as we venerate them. Whether we are wealthy enough to have hand-painted icons or the inexpensive printed variety, what is important is the image itself. If Christ is shown we should treat it as a means to worshipping Him because He is the prototype of each image of Him and through our icons we are able to glorify Him.

Prayer

"Prayer is turning the mind and thoughts toward God. To pray means to stand before God with the mind, mentally to gaze unswervingly at Him, and to converse with Him in reverence, fear and hope."
~ Saint Dimitri of Rostov

There are many great writings on the depths and heights of prayer and I am not equipped to write on such matters. This chapter is concerned with what we understand prayer to be, why it is important and how we should go about it. In the previous chapter we considered the Orthodox understanding of how Christ's incarnation has affected the status and condition of the material world and once more we will see that prayer requires this same perspective when it comes to our bodies.

Prayer is the means by which we encounter God. It is at the very heart of the Church's life and is the means by which members of the Church maintain their bond with one another and with God. It is important to recognise that this bond within the Church is not limited to its members here on earth but also to those in Heaven. We are called to *pray without ceasing* (1Thes. 5 v17) because it is an essential quality of life as a Christian.

We identify two kinds of prayer: corporate and

personal and both are necessary for our spiritual growth. Corporate prayer is the action of the Church when it is gathered for worship and every form of official prayer within the life of the Church is liturgical. We should try to make the hymns and litanies that are sung collectively our own prayers by focussing on the words and allowing the atmosphere of worship to affect our mood and attitude. We should remember our connection with those in church with us and see ourselves as part of the Body of Christ. Christ warned that if we cut ourselves off from the vine we will spiritually wither and die and the sacramental life of the Church must be a regular part of our lives.

But if we only have corporate prayer we are missing the other essential aspect of our spiritual lives. Personal or private prayer is necessary in order for us to be able to truly worship with others; if we live lives empty of personal prayer we cannot hope to pray in any meaningful way when we attend church. Private prayer determines the orientation of our days, it turns us back to God when life makes other demands on us, it helps us to remember God when we are distracted by the world and it gives us strength when our sorrows are great.

Few of us would question the importance of prayer but we should also reflect on the content of our prayer. If we understand this notion of prayer as encounter with God then we see it as an activity that is first and foremost about strengthening our relationship with Him. This may not require words, but the prayers of the Church provide us with a rich resource to draw upon when, as is usually the case, words are needed. Archimandrite Irenei Steenberg describes how he often felt his own words did not quite reflect the full condition of his heart when he was praying, and that at times the great mystery of his inner condition could only be fully expressed through the words of the wise and saintly men and women who have gone before us. The beauty and richness of the prayers of the Church are capable of giving us the means to speak profound truths and realities which our own words may fail to capture and we should make use of them in our personal prayers.

We should not be afraid of bringing to God our whole self, our true self; if we play games with ourselves we create a barrier that can prevent us from meeting with God. We must not allow modern ways of thinking to cause us to be constantly second-guessing ourselves and questioning whether particular prayers are selfish. It is not selfish to ask God to help us grow in our spiritual lives and know Him more deeply and we should also be asking for many other things too. Forgiveness of our sins should be a request that is never far from our lips, it is the foundation of humility and of being able to repent. Unless we become aware of our sinfulness then we are trying to talk to God while hiding behind a mask: we must pour out to him the struggles and failings that exist within us and seek His healing mercy. Our concern for others must also be expressed in our prayers and we must pray knowing that God hears us and has greater love for those we care about than we do. When we pray in this way for others we unite ourselves to God's love and we make it possible for our soul to receive the transforming power of God's grace.

We mentioned above that we believe that the Church is united in Heaven and on earth and for this reason we must also pray for those who have departed this world and be assured that they pray for us. In the early Church it immediately became the practice to seek the intercessions of the saints who had been martyred because it was inconceivable that those who had died for Christ could be anywhere but with God. Saint James tells us to *Pray for one another that you may be healed: for the effectual fervent prayer of a righteous man availeth much* (James 5v16). Accepting this teaching the early Church understood that those who had died in Christ would not only live on but continue to love all members of the Church: and the principle expression of this love is prayer. The saints are spiritually close to us and support us with their intercessions. Just as we approach one another here on earth to ask for prayers for a particular situation so it is natural to seek the prayers of those we believe to now be with God. Similarly it has always been the practice to pray for those who have died that their sins may be forgiven and that they be received into Heaven. We are assured that in God *all are alive* and their nearness to the throne of God only strengthens the power of their prayers. In this way we both confirm and experience the full communion of saints. We also look to the angels for help. These servants of God hear our prayers and are ready to intercede for us.

We do not divide our humanity into sections when we pray: we meet with God as a unity of body and soul. Therefore it is natural for us to use the body in prayer, in bows, making prostrations and signing ourselves with the cross. Christ Himself performed physical actions in His prayer, raising His hands or kneeling, and in His example we see that worship is not solely a spiritual activity but a bodily one too. As we have said the incarnation has made it possible for us to glorify God with our bodies as well as through the physical world around us. When we prostrate ourselves we acknowledge the greatness of God and also our lowliness. Such an act sets our inner state into the right attitude towards God but also helps to focus our attention when we are distracted from our prayer. A prostration is an acknowledgement of God's glory and a request for mercy

But the most common physical action we complete is making the sign of the cross and we will now consider why and how we do this. There are many ways in which making the cross over ourselves can affect us. First it brings to mind that we are in the presence of God, it awakens us to this and can shake us out of the forgetfulness that so easily creeps up on us. The cross itself is a sign of Christ's victory and so when we make it we are bringing to mind His suffering, death and resurrection. This can be a powerful aid when we are despondent or afraid and can remind us to face our own struggles with faith in what He has done. But the cross is more than a symbol; it has spiritual power in itself. The cross is the very means by which Christ overcame death and defeated Satan and so it is a necessary weapon in our battle with the demons. Through this simple action we mark ourselves with Christ's victory and put the cross onto ourselves but it is also a request to God for a blessing.

It is important that we make the cross over ourselves correctly so that we do not treat it with insufficient honour. We must not rush it or wave our hands casually in the air: this approach demonstrates a casual and unacceptable attitude to the cross. We start at the head and then move from right shoulder to the left for many reasons and different Church Fathers will stress different ones. First we acknowledge that Christ sits at the right hand of the Father (Romans 8 v34), but we also recall Christ's warning that at judgement when the sheep and the goats are separated the righteous will move to God's right. For these reasons we also only ever cross ourselves with our right hand and we move the hand down from head to chest as a symbol of Christ's descent from heaven to earth.

When we face the priest in church he blesses us by making the cross from left to right and so our hands reflect the movement of his. In the late twelfth century under Pope Innocent III western Christians reversed the direction they make the sign of the cross.

The arrangement of our fingers is also significant. We touch the thumb and first two fingers together (index and middle) in remembrance of the Holy Trinity while the other two fingers folded against the palm signify Christ's two natures. Touching the head demonstrates the intention to offer our thoughts and will to God, while the chest represents our heart and feelings while the shoulders represent our strength which is offered to the service of God. There are different attitudes to bowing when making the cross: someone once told me they were reprimanded by a monk in America for bowing when crossing themself because it bent the cross while others believe a small bow is appropriate to receiving the blessing. Which ever practice is your local custom is the one to follow.

There are particular times when it is the custom to make the sign of the cross in corporate worship, such as when the Holy Trinity is mentioned in the prayers or when agreement is being expressed with the words of the priest. It is traditional to sign oneself when the bread and wine has been changed into Christ's Body and Blood and also before and after receiving Holy Communion. The sign of the cross also helps to make us able to hear and receive the Gospel message in the Divine Liturgy. As we have mentioned previously, it is the custom to also make the sign of the cross when venerating icons. But there are many other occasions when we should do so and we consider here just a few of them.

We make the sign of the cross as we enter a church to mark our passing from the world into the holy space before the altar. Doing so helps to remember our unworthiness but also the great blessing we have in being welcomed by God like the father greeting the returning prodigal son. The cross declares our identity as Christians and our belonging in church.

In Orthodox countries it has been a tradition to make the sign of the cross over oneself when passing a church. There are stories from the Soviet period of Russian history when old ladies would risk arrest by crossing themselves in the streets or even on buses as they passed churches. This is done because the churches contain the Body and Blood of Christ reserved for the sick, and the faithful cannot pass by without reverently honouring the One Who is present.

Other times include before and after eating, before beginning prayer, before embarking on a journey or any action that may be dangerous or important. In fact it is appropriate to make the sign of the cross whenever we need to ask God's blessing and as long as it is not done ostentatiously in order to attract attention to show pious we are we should always be ready to turn to this sacred action. One final comment however is that on Mount Athos the monks limit the occasions on which they cross themselves as it can become distracting to others around them if they are performing such actions too frequently. This thinking should also affect our own practice as we should always be seeking to be as courteous and humble in church as we can be.

One other tradition within Orthodoxy is the use of the *Jesus Prayer* which is the reciting of the words *Lord Jesus Christ, Son of God, have mercy on me a sinner.* There is a wealth of material on this topic in *The Philokalia* where instruction is often accompanied by the warning that the practice of its use should be done under the direction of an experienced spiritual guide. This is because some people are not spiritually or psychologically ready for this form of prayer. The use of the *Jesus Prayer* developed because we believe that the name of Jesus Christ has spiritual power since it is a divine name. It is not a form of meditation or mantra and should never be used as such. It requires us to focus carefully on the words and allow their meaning to bring us into a deeper awareness of Christ's presence and many have attested to its ability to help transform the human heart.

Finally we should reflect on a few practical points when it comes to our prayers. If we are attempting to improve the way we pray we should ensure that a few basic principles are being followed. The first is that we have a regular pattern of prayer. We should reflect on our work and other demands and identify times in the day that we can protect as times for prayer without interruption. Building a life of prayer requires a certain amount of discipline and developing a regular pattern will help us in this. We are creatures of habit and while we fight to release ourselves from bad habits we should also be working to learn good ones. A further point on this is that we should never trust our prayer to times when we feel like praying. This approach is unhelpful since our feelings are not to be trusted. It is often at the times when we have to force ourselves to pray that God blesses us more deeply. If we find we are waking up at night because of stress then use the opportunity to pray and defeat the negative feelings that may be causing you problems.

Making prostrations and the sign of the cross may not immediately feel natural but once we have gotten over these kinds of self-conscious feelings they quickly become natural to us. These physical actions will also help us when we do not particularly feel like praying as they can often invigorate us and prompt us to focus on what we are doing. The body should also be given an opportunity to calm itself if we have come from a rushed or demanding activity. We must always remember that we are body and soul and prayer requires that our whole self be offered.

As a last thought we should remember that it is possible for prayer to go wrong. If we begin to treat our prayers as an obligation or allow resentment to creep into our hearts then it is not prayer that we will be doing. If we permit our pride to swell because we are so pleased at how long we have begun to pray for we should see the danger we are in and run to confession. And of course let us never forget that the one thing the demons want us never to do is pray. They will do everything to prevent us from spending time with God; by reminding us of good works we should be doing, by disturbing us or throwing distractions in our way. But if we establish a pattern to our life we will overcome these temptations. There have also been accounts of people believing they are having visions or seeing lights when in prayer and the Church Fathers warn us all to reject such things. If we hold on to the knowledge of how sinful we are we will know that we are not worthy of such visions and the demons will not be able to mislead us. Pray with simplicity and faith and trust that God hears every word and measures every heart beat.

Fasting

"Fasting is the change of every part of our life, because the sacrifice of the fast is not the abstinence but the distancing from sins. Therefore, whoever limits the fast to the deprivation of food, he is the one who, in reality, abhors and ridicules the fast."
~ Saint John Chrysostom

Before Christ began His ministry which would lead to His crucifixion and resurrection He went into the desert for forty days to fast and pray. He was not only preparing Himself but also setting an example which we are to follow: we are called to fast in order to live the way God wants us to but also to be ready for our resurrection. Christians have always understood fasting to be an essential part of the spiritual life in order that we can bring ourselves back to God and live in communion with Him. In this chapter we will first look at how the practice developed within the life of the Church and then reflect on its purpose for us today.

Fasting as a moral discipline existed in Jewish life both in terms of when it should be done and what foods could be eaten. It was clearly recognised as an act of devotion and Christ refers to the fasting amongst Jews on a number of occasions. The first Christians continued with this

159

practice and developed a pattern which in some ways reflected the Jewish approach. Jews for example fasted on Mondays and Thursdays and in the Church the practice became to fast on Wednesdays and Fridays (because these were the days when Christ was plotted against and then crucified). Similarly the development of the Christian calendar mirrored the Jewish practice of having annual feast days which required periods of preparation involving fasting. Over time there has been variation in the Church's approach to fasting in terms of what is eaten and the length of the duration of the fasts, and even today with the rules of fasting established there is some local difference over what is done: for example it is seen by some local churches as acceptable to drink beer when the fast specifies that wine must not be consumed. Again some local churches will permit celebrations of local saints to take place when the Church is observing a fast.

One major difference however, between the Jewish and Christian practice was over which foods are permitted. While the Torah forbids a range of foods because they are judged as unclean, Christian understanding is that all food is permitted on a fast-free day and that degrees of strictness are applied to the eating of meat and other animal products (dairy), fish, wine and oil depending on which fast is being observed. Both Judaism and Islam apply the Law of Moses in seeing certain foods as forbidden at all times and Muslims also reject the consumption of alcohol. These different approaches reflect a theological difference in that Christians believe the whole of creation is called to redemption in Christ and so nothing is regarded as ritually unclean in this way. Black pudding, or blood sausage, is not eaten by Orthodox Christians because it is the consumption of blood.

Christ's criticism of the Pharisees was that they had turned the practice of fasting into a legalistic observance: it had become an outward show of fasting and had lost its inner meaning. Saint Symeon the New Theologian tells us that *Fasting, aided by vigil, penetrates and softens hardness of heart.* In these few words Saint Symeon expresses two great truths: that fasting must be accompanied by prayer but also that it has a direct impact on our inner state when performed with the right attitude. Fasting is never performed as an end in itself, in this sense it is not a virtue, but enables the one who fasts to develop self-control in order that they may become more virtuous.

Once more we remind ourselves that we have a holistic understanding of what it means to be a human being, we are both body and soul. However we recognise that in our fallen state the soul is often under the control of bodily appetites and impulses. We do not believe that the impulse to eat and drink is in any way evil, quite the opposite, it is something which enables us to respond by giving nourishment to our bodies so that we continue to live. Fasting is not a rejection of the body or its needs; it is a restoration of it to its proper condition as the servant of the soul. Therefore we can see fasting as a form of liberation. True freedom is liberation from the enslavement to habits and impulses, an idea which flies in the face of modern philosophy. Western Christians live within a secular culture which elevates the fulfilment of our impulses and desires to a false status and mistakes it for freedom. But true Christianity teaches that only when we are able to deny these impulses within ourselves can we know freedom; only when we try to deny these impulses do we discover how powerful their hold over us can be. We must see that the way we are living in the twenty-first century is abnormal; we have become distorted by the lack of restraint over our passions and allowed the body to reign over us. The passions are themselves a result of the distortion of our bodily needs which have a God-given purpose but have been released from our control.

Our desire for food is perhaps the basic of all our bodily drives and in all creatures that share this physical need for nutrition we see a desire to fulfil it. But uncontrolled appetites weaken our ability to control other desires and impulses and the patristic writers place an emphasis on guarding ourselves against gluttony as a vital part of our spiritual development. There is in all of us a tendency to choose comfort and ease, and laziness quickly results from it. The Fathers understood this and taught that it is in God's mercy that He has given us the cycle of fasting as a kind of medicine against this ailment.

Fasting is to be seen beyond the mere control of our consumption of food. We must not allow ourselves to start thinking of food as somehow evil; there are a growing number of people suffering from mental illness because of this error. Instead we must see our fasting within the context of our desire to ask God to restore that which has been distorted to a state of goodness. We exist in a state of rebellion against God, and this evil comes from the heart. Our self-denial is intended to bring the whole self, body, mind and spirit back into communion with God, to offer the heart to God and ask for His grace. We should see fasting as part of the purification of our heart so that it is in a condition which permits it to receive God's grace: by setting loose the desires of our fallen self we pollute the heart and prevent ourselves from receiving God's grace. This requires a state of harmony to exist between the soul and body so that there is a balance in the forces within the heart in the way that God intended. Saint Symeon the New Theologian reminds us that only when we fill our intellect with moral goodness and beauty will it be drawn and united to the spiritual self while the intellect filled with ugliness, sin and materialism will be united with the fallen, corrupted self.

When we fast we can become hungry and tired which can lead us to a greater sense of dependency on God. When we eat and drink to contentment we can quickly become over-confident and satisfied and lose our sense of need of His help. Our consumption of food reflects Christ's warning about the danger of being rich if we wish to enter Heaven: worldly wealth can lead us into a false self-reliance just as too much food can. We must be thankful for the gift of the Holy Spirit and do all that we can to nurture and protect this precious gift. The virtues that please the Holy Spirit are the fruit of a disciplined life and spiritual struggle.

Christ's example also reminds us that fasting is a kind of desert where we go to meet with God. The desert is a place that is separate from normal life and our normal way of living. It is a place of seriousness and repentance, a place of estrangement from evil where we must face the truth of ourselves. In the desert we are humbled by our physical needs which should teach us humility of spirit. In the desert we abstain not just from food but from sin, we reject self-love and embrace a kind of living martyrdom where we die to our old self and embrace the eternal life of God. Being illuminated does not just give us the means by which we can see the true path where we are to walk, it gives us the strength to walk it. Fasting is an expression of our self-sacrifice, a taking up of our cross in order that our whole self may be sanctified.

We will now address the question of how we should fast and what the practicalities are for us. The first thing to say is we must avoid anything that may lead us to a state of pride. As we shall see, the Church's rules for the fasts are such that few of us live up to them and this should be a useful source of humility. In the patristic writings on this subject we repeatedly hear the call to follow the royal or middle way. We are instructed to ensure that our bodily needs are met and an over-enthusiastic desire for strictness in fasting can lead to spiritual and physical ill health. There are numerous accounts of how the demons have used someone's idealism to break their health or fill them with pride at their great ascetical feats. Fasting must be part of our seeking for fullness of life and must not become an outward display of pseudo-sanctity. Of course Christ also tells us that fasting and prayer are great weapons against the demons and through them their evil presence can be removed. Many converts to Orthodoxy are rightly inspired by the lives of great monastic saints but the danger can be that they try to emulate the outer practices while not pursuing the inner dimension of their lives. The sad truth is that we in the West are living in a culture that is so alien to the natural life of traditional Orthodox countries that we can have a distorted perception of the distinction between monasticism and the life of the laity. Asceticism is intended for all people, monastic and lay, the rules about eating meat would be nonsense otherwise, since monks never eat flesh. Our work and daily lives are not structured around the feasts and fasts of the Church in the way people experienced life in the past and so our internal rhythms and sense of time are no longer in sync with the cycles of the Church year in the same way. This is important to remember because even those who enter the monastic life in the West may still have aspects of their inner life that are completely alien to true Orthodox living. Therefore we must be realistic about what we can achieve: this is not to say we should not strive to do more than we have done previously, but that we must see our capabilities for what they are. It can be extremely damaging for us if we set out with unrealistic intentions only to find that within a few weeks we have failed miserably. Asceticism is really about living a life that is purposeful, that is ordered and controlled.

I do not intend to list all the various dates and periods of fasting, these can be found in the calendars sold in our churches and there are also versions available for free on the internet. Not everyone is expected to fast. Young infants, the very old, the sick, those who are pregnant and those nursing babies are exempted. If someone is taking medication that affects their ability to fast they should speak to their priest. The main periods of fasting are: Lent, Holy Week and Pascha, the Apostle's Fast, the Dormition Fast, the Nativity Fast and also the Eve of Theophany, the Exaltation of the Cross and the Beheading of Saint John the Baptist. There is a balance to the year in that as well as there being four great periods of fasting there are four seasons when fasting is forbidden. These are the Nativity of Theophany, the week following the Sunday of the Publican and Pharisee, Bright Week (the week after Pascha) and Trinity Week (the week between Pentecost and the Sunday of All Saints.

When we approach the fasts we should identify those aspects of our lives where we can also limit other activities such as watching television or listening to music and there should be an accompanying increase in activities such as prayer, reading and participation in collective worship. When we fast we should completely ignore the extent to which anyone else is fasting and if we find ourselves judging others we should immediately take it as a sign that we have a sinful state of mind.

The Church does not permit us to fast on Sundays because this is the day of Christ's resurrection and should be reflected in our joy. Fasting should be a way in which we adopt a sorrowful state of mourning over our sins and this is inappropriate when we are celebrating the resurrection. The Church does call us to fast before receiving Holy Communion in order that we be physically able to receive Him not only through our stomach but also to help us prepare ourselves inwardly. If an infant is to receive Holy Communion the parents should ensure that feeding takes place two or three hours before the child receives. Every one else should fast from the previous midnight and those who are married should abstain from marital relations on the night before receiving. The fasting rules also require couples to abstain from sexual relations on Wednesdays and Fridays and during the fasting periods. As a bare minimum couples should abstain before receiving Holy Communion and during Holy Week.

Earlier I pointed out that many people fail to fulfil all of the fasting rules. How many of us, for example, observe the rule to eat only two full meals during the first five days of the first week of Great Lent? If this comment applies to us we should not be discouraged but recognise that there are people who manage all of the fasting rules and this may help us to avoid becoming proud over the little that we achieve.

Finally we should remember that it is possible to keep the letter of the law when it comes to fasting and fail to keep its spirit. It is possible to fast and still practice gluttony. Our instructions to fast are not a rule book to be slavishly followed: fasting is a means to our healing and the rules are something we can measure ourselves against and give ourselves something more to strive towards. Orthodoxy rejects any kind of legalistic approach to life and we must never imagine that our efforts, however great they may be, are what achieve our salvation. Fasting is like the turning of the soil, unless God gives us the seed, rain and sunshine nothing can grow, but if the farmer does not work the land even the most fruitful seeds will produce a poor harvest.

Monasticism

"A monk is a man who has freed his intellect from attachment to material things and by means of self-control, love, psalmody and prayer cleaves to God."
~ Saint Maximos the Confessor

Monasticism is an essential part of the Orthodox Church. Uniquely among Christian traditions the spirituality and the doctrines of Orthodoxy have been upheld and defended by monks and as has often been repeated, for the Church as a whole to be healthy, monasticism must be healthy. But ask most people what is meant by a monk and the answer will often involve descriptions of the outward ordering of their lives: how they dress, how their days are structured and so on. But the quotation above points to the truth of monasticism, that regardless of its outer appearance monasticism is an inner condition which is concerned with repentance and purification. As we shall see it is this inner reality that is the true essence of monasticism and which is so important for the spiritual life of the whole Body. We will first consider the historical development of monasticism before reflecting on its importance for the whole Church.

There is a cliché that states that with the Edict of Milan in 313 A.D. under Emperor Constantine the legalisation of Christianity encouraged a less committed attitude amongst many Christians which in turn prompted devout disciples of Christ to seek the isolation of the Egyptian wilderness in order to practise their faith with greater sincerity. While there is some truth to this version the full history is more complicated. In fact as early as the middle of the second century some Christian writers were noting a moral decline amongst many communities and this led to some individuals reacting against any notion of compromise in their faith. They chose lives of chastity, poverty and prayer and though they remained within towns and cities they tried to set themselves apart from the surrounding society. They took as their examples the Theotokos and Saint John the Baptist and recognised their choice of celibacy as being above nature, enabling them to strive to live like the angels. We shall return to this issue of celibacy shortly.

It was around the middle of the third century that this desire for an uncompromising Christian life led the first Christians to move out into the deserts. Some chose to live alone while others lived near to one another so that they could gather for common worship on Sundays and on feast days. The first men to do this were called *anchorites* which comes from *anchoresis* which means *departure* because they were recognised initially as those who had departed from the world. Another term used to describe them was *hermits* which comes from *eremos* meaning desert: this word later came to apply to those monks who lived in isolation even away from other monks. Later they would all be given the name *monks* which comes from *monos* meaning alone. Recognised as *The Father of Monasticism* Saint Anthony the Great who, though not the first monk (he went to the desert around 285 A.D.) is recognised as the one who inspired many by his ascetic life and later by his teachings. Saint Anthony's life of isolation is seen as the model for hermits, but it is Saint Pachomios of Egypt (280 – 346 A.D.) who founded the pattern of cenobitic living where all property is held in common and where the community lives under the authority of an elder. It is this form of monasticism that is now most common because of the inherent spiritual dangers of living alone if one is not spiritually mature enough to face it.

Saint Basil the Great (303 – 379 AD) produced two works, *Great Rules* and *Brief Rules* which further regulated the life of monastics and it should also be noted that he was very critical of the isolated life of hermits. Later Saint Benedict adapted many of Saint Basil's ideas for his own rules which became so influential in the West.

Two further important figures we should note are Saint Symeon the New Theologian (949 – 1022 A.D.) and Saint Gregory Palamas (1296 – 1359 A.D.) who both had an important role with regard to monasticism but also defended the truths of

Orthodoxy. Both of these saints recognised the reality of direct experience of God within the sacramental life of the Church. Saint Gregory explained the doctrines of God's essence and energies because of attacks on this belief and, as a result, the heart of Orthodox spirituality is centred on the striving for purification of the self in order to encounter God in a personal and tangible way. While this sort of thinking is to be found amongst fringe mystics of the Roman traditions it is for Orthodox the basis of the spiritual life for all members of the Church. Saint Gregory recognised the link between the hesychastic tradition and the light revealed on Mount Tabor at the Transfiguration. As we shall see in a final chapter, it is our transfiguration that is the true purpose of existence.

The centre of Orthodox monasticism is Mount Athos, a Greek peninsula jutting out into the Aegean Sea. Monastics have been living there since before the tenth century but the Great Republic of Monks is recognised as beginning in 983 A.D. with the building of The Great Lavra by a monk called Athanasius. The community soon attracted Christians from numerous Orthodox countries and today monastic life thrives on the Holy Mountain with a truly pan-Orthodox presence.

Monasticism is rooted in the writings of Saint Paul who teaches us that though marriage is a blessing from God those who choose celibacy make a sacrifice of what is good so that they may live, as has been described, above nature. It is important for us to remember that marriage and celibacy are both means by which God has enabled us to enter the Kingdom of God. But whereas marriage belongs to this world, the life of celibacy is a foretaste of the eternal life to come since the monks choose to live like the angels. Christ teaches us in the gospels that after the resurrection we will not marry and the monastic life is a faithful anticipation of what is to come.

Monastics enter a state characterised as one of *joyful mourning*, one of grief for the world illuminated by the mercy and forgiveness of Christ. Monasticism is in no way opposed to the world, on the contrary monks hold all of us in constant prayer and we can be assured that without their intercession so many of the calamities that we witness around us would be so much worse. But there is a detachment that is maintained within the life of the monk, they must be *in the world but not of the world*. This is because the life of monasticism is one of stillness centred on continuous awareness of God. They remind us that the Christian life is not fulfilled through outward observance but is the inner condition of a heart given unreservedly to God.

Monasticism has contributed to the life of the Church in a number of practical ways beyond the support of prayer and the spiritual example given to us by monastic saints. In the early Church it was the monks who gave credibility to the Christian faith along with the martyrs. Both groups exhibited in their lives the truths they professed with their lips. Their witness had a profound effect on the pagan cultures in which they lived and died. Many monks have been at the front line in the battle against heresy and have been called out of the deserts in order to proclaim the truth. For example monks of the Studion monastery re-entered the world in order to defeat iconoclasm and they were able to make clear not only the false teachings of heresy but also the indivisible link between doctrine and theology and the spiritual life. The truths of the Church are not mere intellectual arguments but the fruit of life lived with God: they are revelation.

Many monks have also returned to the world in order to share their spiritual experiences and offer guidance to the Church. Saint Basil emphasised the role of monks within the mission of the Church and this has been further benefited by the education offered by monks through history: the education of the clergy has had vital support from monasteries. During the expansion of the Ottoman Empire monks also ensured that faith and culture were maintained under Islamic occupation where it might otherwise have been obliterated.

In recent decades there has been a renewal of interest in monasticism which may be driven by a reaction against the prevailing materialism of western culture. As modern life pushes people further away from what is natural, wholesome and healthy so there is for many a desire for an authentic way of living. Orthodox Christianity offers this way, but there are many who still seek the uncompromising life of the desert. In Orthodox countries it is still the norm for lay people to visit and spend time in monasteries in order to regain a clear perspective on their lives and seek advice about problems they may be having. Monasticism is a mystery that can only be understood through direct experience, but its essential nature is the same existence we are all called to find: one lived with trust in God, hope of the Kingdom to come, and repentance of our sins.

The Theotokos

"Anyone who does not admit that holy Mary is the Mother of God is out of touch with the Godhead."
~ Saint Gregory Nazianus

Mary the Mother of our Lord has a vital and central place in God's plan of salvation. The Mother of God is the means by which Christ took flesh and became one of us. Her role is not passive but required her active agreement; our salvation was made possible because this young woman was obedient to God. Consequently we celebrate her role in Christ's incarnation but we also recognise her as a powerful source of intercession because of her position as one of us while having such an intimate relationship with our Saviour. In this brief reflection we will identify what the Orthodox Church believes about her and how we express it in our worship.

In the *Akathist To Our Most Holy Lady The Theotokos* we pray:
Rejoice, heavenly ladder by which God came down; Rejoice bridge that conveyest us
        from earth to Heaven!
In these few words we begin to see how the Church understands the Theotokos. The images of

177

a ladder and a bridge emphasise her role as the link between the human and the divine, because in her the heavenly and earthly realms of existence come into union in a new and glorious way: Christ the eternal Logos descended to our world through her flesh that we may ascend to His heavenly kingdom. It is in her womb that the divine and human natures are united in Christ Who took His flesh from hers. She is in this all humanity since she shares without any kind of difference our humanity.

While Roman Catholics have dared to create detailed and systematic theological explanations of her role the Orthodox Church has understood much about her as mystery. As a result the Church has instead relayed its faith about her within its liturgical life. In the hymns and prayers of our liturgies we constantly return to her place in our salvation and many times we find her described in symbols and images. The idea of her being a ladder is just one way of conveying what she has done for us, other images include descriptions of her as a *temple,* a *doorway* and a *chariot.* Again in the Akathist we say:

Rejoice, all holy chariot of Him who sitteth upon the cherubim: Rejoice all-glorious
temple of Him Who is above the seraphim.

These kinds of images come from the Church's approach to interpreting the Bible known as t*ypology.* This involves seeing time and events not just in terms of linear procession but through cycles and connections. In this way what may occur in the

Old Testament becomes a type or pattern through which later events can be understood. It also means that some events can only ever be truly understood through what follows because they do not find completion in one moment in time but are fulfilled through what happens later. Two particular examples of this approach that apply to the Theotokos are the burning bush and Eve.

When Moses saw the vision of Christ in the burning bush he witnessed the fire of God which did not consume the bush. This has a number of interpretations but it only finds its full meaning in Mary who conceived and gave birth to Christ without the destruction of her virginity. The issue of her virginity is something we will return to but let us turn first to the second example, that of Eve.

As early as the second century the title *Second Eve* was being used to describe the Theotokos. The story in Genesis assumes a new and deeper meaning when we understand the role of Eve as a type for Mary. Where Eve was disobedient to God the Theotokos is obedient, and so as sin and death entered into the world through Eve's actions, so Christ and His redemption enter the cosmos through Mary who listened not to the words of a serpent but to the proclamation of an angel.

The words of the Archangel Gabriel at the Annunciation give us further insight into Mary's role when we apply typology. Gabriel says to her *The Holy Spirit will come upon you and the power of the Most high will overshadow you.* Two key images are offered to us: the first is of the Holy Spirit moving over the water at creation and the second is of the tabernacle erected by Moses; let us consider each in turn. We are reminded of God's creative power and how what the Theotokos agrees to is mirrored in the first act of creation at the beginning of the world. Through her obedience God's creative power will make things new, make things good, as they were in the beginning. And the second image comes from the idea of God's power *overshadowing* her. This is the image we find in Exodus when Moses constructed the tent (tabernacle) in which God dwelt that He might be present in the midst of His people. So we see Mary as a new tabernacle in which God's glory dwells and through whom the Church has God in our midst. Beyond the imagery of typology we must also recognise the significance of the titles given to Mary and how she is our greatest intercessor before Christ.

The title *Theotokos* means *God-Bearer* or *One Who Gives Birth to God*. This is such an important title because it confirms our faith in the incarnation of God Himself: by calling Mary Theotokos we are identifying Christ as truly being the Second Person of the Holy Trinity. This means that the One Who is eternally Begotten of the Father is now born of a woman. At times when the truth of Christ's identity has been attacked by heretics the title Theotokos has been an important proclamation of the Church's faith. We believe that within her womb was contained the very God Who is eternal and beyond all limits and that through her humanity He united Himself to us; God the Creator entered His creation.

The title *Mother of God* is often used interchangeably with *Theotokos* but the two have subtle differences. While the Greek term emphasises her place within the Christological doctrine of the Church, the former title communicates her human connection to Christ. It is ironic that the Roman Catholics have tended to use the term *Mother of God* while often attempting to remove the human aspects of her experience as a mother. In Orthodox hymns we often focus on her grief and suffering to emphasise her full humanity. In the Church's understanding it is crucial that we see her as absolutely and completely human in every sense that we are, including the details of her conception. Through the doctrine of the *Immaculate Conception* (which only became official Roman Catholic doctrine in 1854) Latin Christians have separated the Theotokos from us by removing her from the full reality of sin and temptation. Mary's obedience to God is only true obedience if she knows the full temptation to choose otherwise and so the Latin approach robs her of the fullness of her human sanctity. Of course Roman Catholics are forced to create the idea of her immaculate conception because of their false teaching on original sin (maintaining that we are all born with an inherited guilt as a result of Adam's sin rather than simply with the consequences of that sin).

Since the Theotokos is forever the Mother of God she is recognised as having a powerful role in praying for all humanity but particularly the Church. One title given to her is *protector* and Christians through out the ages have sought her help in times of need. One famous example comes from the seventh century when Constantinople was under military attack by the Persians. The citizens of the city prayed for her help and many witnesses testified to seeing her at the walls during the fighting defending the Christians. Once more it is her full humanity that gives her such concern for us: countless ordinary Christians can testify to the reality of her intervention. Once more we turn to the words of the Akathist which says:

Rejoice, acceptable incense of intercession: Rejoice, propitiation of all the world!

One final aspect that we will focus on is her virginity. Calling the Theotokos *Ever-Virgin* is important for Christological reasons but also because of her importance in the lives of monastics.

In the second century many of the traditions concerning the Theotokos were included in a volume called the *Protoevangelium of James*. From this work many of the Church's hymns drew details about her life and meaning. In it we read how the Theotokos was presented to the Temple when she was three years old and for the next nine years lived an ascetic existence entirely focussed on God.

This period came to an end when she was betrothed to Joseph in order to care for his children from a previous marriage. Saint Gregory Palamas taught that during these nine years the Theotokos lived as the first hesychast; and subsequently she was recognised as the great model of a life of prayer for all monastics. Within this understanding her virginity is held as the ideal for all hesychasts and it is understood both in terms of her physical and spiritual state. In the Beatitudes Christ teaches *Blessed are the pure in heart for they shall see God* and so the Orthodox tradition is that in this blessed state of prayer and purity the Theotokos communed with God in a profound and mystical manner. We see here the two reasons for the level of purity she attained which made her able to receive Christ in her womb: first the grace of God but second the life of holiness which she followed. But the Theotokos' virginity is also crucial for our understanding of Christ's incarnation. Without the miraculous conception in a virgin's womb Christ could not have been God. It is the absence of a human father in the conception that demonstrates the uniqueness of Christ and His divine nature. Having given her body to be the vessel of God's incarnation it is unthinkable that she would then have sexual relations since her flesh had been sanctified and dedicated for the purpose of the incarnation: she was truly a living temple dedicated and set aside for that role. It is similarly unthinkable for the Orthodox that a woman chosen by God and blessed with such grace would return to the world of the flesh. On Mount Athos the monks speak of her as the living fulfilment of theosis, one who has become transfigured by the Holy Spirit. Her flesh was truly made holy by God and through her obedience and it is not something she cast off after Christ's birth.

Finally we should mention the Feast of the Dormition and Orthodox belief about the end of the Theotokos' life. Roman Catholics have made concrete doctrines about the details of her dormition and it must be said that there are many Orthodox who accept the content of these doctrines. But the Church has not made it a matter of dogma that the Theotokos was assumed into Heaven before her death or even the exact details of what happened to her body. Once more we accept that some historical events have aspects of mystery over which there is no requirement to make dogmatic statements. We do believe that her body which had been blessed to carry Christ was not permitted to decay but was taken into Heaven. We also believe that her death was accompanied by miraculous events such as the gathering of the Apostles from many different locations in order to be present at her dormition.

From this brief reflection we should understand that Orthodox devotion to the Theotokos is in no way a sentimental or unnecessary addition to the faith, it is a crucial expression of our faith. The incarnation is not a myth which has no location in history, but a historical reality rooted in the life of the Theotokos. She is the human being offered up to God by creation, the one creature made worthy to make it possible for every one of us to find salvation. And having given her womb that God may dwell there, she nurtured and protected the holy child to manhood so that He might reveal to the whole world the truth of God. As the Akathist says:

Rejoice, Thou who didst extinguish the furnace of error. Rejoice, thou who didst enlighten the initiates of the Trinity.

The Saints

"Cleave to the saints, for they who cleave to them shall be made holy."
~ Saint Clement of Rome

The saints are proof that even ordinary creatures like us can enter Heaven and be made holy. In this way they are one of the ways that God blesses and reassures us. They pray with us and for us and the Church has always taught that we share our lives with them as a single Body both on earth and in Heaven. In Christ we are united and the bond between us cannot be destroyed by physical death: for all who have the life of Christ within them there is an eternal bond that is more powerful than space, time and death itself. Saint John of Kronstadt says *We live together with them in the house of the Heavenly Father, only in different parts of it. We live in the earthly, they in the heavenly half.* We believe that our unity reflects the unity between the Persons of the Holy Trinity despite our failings and sinfulness. For the saints in Heaven however, love is not limited by sin, it is magnified beyond our imagination and so their concern for us in our earthly trials is all the greater. In Heaven the saints do not become numbed to the realities of life on earth, they know only too well the difficulties of our lives and intercede for us.

From the earliest times Christians understood this bond and expressed it in their worship. As many gave themselves to martyrdom it was unthinkable that they could be anywhere but with God, but similarly it made no sense to think that the love they felt for their fellow Christians would come to an end now that they were in Heaven. They pray for us as they did while on earth but with greater power. Saint John Chrysostom encourages us to seek the intercessions of the saints because he says *they have a special boldness before the throne of God* (boldness in the sense of knowing they are freely welcomed by God without sin or hesitation).

But it is important to understand what this means: it is not spiritualism. Those who consult mediums wish to interact with the dead and receive messages: a practice condemned in the Holy Scriptures and by Christian Tradition. We are not in contact with the dead; in fact many theologians have stated that the saints do not hear our voices as we seek their prayers. Many holy people are given knowledge of things by God in this life: for example many saints (such as Saint Paisios of Mount Athos) know people's names when they meet them and have insight into their concerns before they have been told anything. This vision of events or circumstances is a gift from God and it is in this way that the saints are granted awareness of our request for intercession. In the New Testament we are told that there is only one mediator between man and God and that is Jesus Christ. The saints do not mediate; they act as supplicants before God on our behalf. They do not possess their own divine grace nor can they impart it to us from themselves, the transforming grace they receive is from God. The saints do not save or redeem us but as our friends they pray for us. Christ, too, knows from His own experience the trials of human life and so we must not imagine that the saints are closer to us than God or in any way understand us more than God. Neither should we fall into the trap of imagining that the saints are somehow more approachable than God: they are not substitutes for God. But the Holy Scriptures assure us that the prayers of a righteous man are powerful and we see countless examples of God's people seeking the prayers of those living holy lives (even Saint Paul requested those he wrote to, to pray for him).

Let us now consider how the Church recognises someone as a saint, what types of people are called saints, and why the relics of saints and places associated with them are treated as holy. We will then reflect on what it means to venerate saints and what more beyond their prayers they do for us.

A saint is really someone who has been made holy by God. Of course God is the only source of all holiness and so the saints are those who have received from God such grace that they have been sanctified both in soul and body (this is important when we think about their relics). This is not a random occurrence but is made possible through their obedience to God and the sincerity of their love for Him. The Church does have an official system of recognition of the saints which requires a form of encyclical letter from the Ecumenical Patriarch but inclusion of saints in local traditions is often far more informal. The reality is that it is not the Church who makes saints but God, and so awareness of someone's saintliness is a gift to us rather than a change in the person's condition. It is often the love expressed by a local community who knew the saint that establishes veneration of them and the Church hierarchy really confirms what the people already believe. On a more personal level someone may be so convinced of someone's sanctity that immediately after their death members of the family may seek their intercessions. In Heaven there are many more saints than are recognised on earth whose hidden holy lives were known only to God.

In his epistles Saint Paul uses the term *saints* to refer to all the members of the Church but over time specific categories of people have been identified as saints: they are the Apostles, the martyrs, the Prophets of the Old Testament, the Fathers of the Church (hierarchs and teachers) and the just (whether clergy, monastic or laity). In all of these groups the essential quality is being united with God and in the lives of the saints we see great diversity in their lifestyles and circumstances. It is not the outward circumstances of their lives that made them saints but the way they chose to be disciples of Christ and give themselves completely to His will.

The early Church would meet on the anniversary of a saint's entry into Heaven and when possible they would do so at the saint's tomb or where their relics were kept: Saint John Chrysostom tells us that the tombs of the saints are filled with a special blessing. Through this we see that even the physical space where martyrdom took place is sanctified. Similarly early monastics settled in the desert of Egypt at those places associated with holy events in history such as when Moses struck the rock to release water and where he was given the vision of the burning bush. Many churches in Palestine were built where important events happened in the life of Christ and through their proximity with the place Christians believe they are brought closer to God in their prayer. But it is not just the places that are important; we also have physical remains of the saints. Every consecrated Orthodox church contains within its altar saints' relics. Here we reflect again on the theme of our belief in the sanctification of the physical universe. It is not only the souls of the saints that have been made holy but also their bodies. Many saints have achieved such a profound state of holiness that their physical remains are incorrupt after death. We believe that God grants us these signs to strengthen us in our faith and it is truly a joy-filled experience to be able to venerate one of God's faithful servants whose body has been untouched by decay. Just as the body is the temple of the Holy Spirit while we live it remains so after death. Though the soul has temporarily left the body (until the Day of Resurrection) it remains changed by the power of God's presence. When the body has been used in the service of God and as a means of attaining grace it mysteriously retains the effect of God's redemption and continues to be a link to the saint. If the soul and body have worked in harmony for God then the soul has no need to flee from its physical partner as so many may want to do at death. Since the soul and body will be resurrected together the link between them remains strong and so being close to a saint's relics brings us closer to the one now in God's presence in Heaven. We believe that water that is blessed can be used to bless people and objects so how much more blessed are we by the bones that were alive with the grace-filled soul of a saint. The fact that the body will rise to Christ's call is also a reason why we treat the dead body with such respect and the belief in this link between body and soul also makes sense of what we do at funeral services. Many Protestants are taught that such practices are more recent innovations but we read that the bones of Saint Polycarp were collected and treated *as more precious than gold* by the Church in the middle of the second century.

When we describe these activities it is important to distinguish between the veneration offered to the saints and the worship that is offered to God alone.

In English the exact definition of *worship* means to *give worth to* or to recognise the value of something or someone. This is why even in traditional Anglican marriage services the groom promises to worship his wife: no one ever imagines his intention is to build a shrine to her or make her into an idol. But as we have seen earlier, we understand *worship* as meaning more than this in a religious sense; it is the acknowledgement of God in His glory as the one source of all life and being. We do not attribute such things to the saints; rather we are acknowledging what God has done in them. Just as we described the way we glorify God through icons, so too we may say that the saints are living icons through whom God is glorified. They are human beings just like us but human beings who have demonstrated the way God wants all of us to live. God remains the prototype of all holiness and the saints have had His likeness restored within them just as all of us must struggle to rediscover our true identity as beings created in God's image.

Every time we repent and resist evil impulses we benefit both ourselves but also all people who share our one humanity. Therefore we should look to the saints with gratitude because they have battled so courageously to contribute to the condition that is common to us all. But we should find encouragement too in the awareness that we are surrounded by a *cloud of witnesses* who have run the race that we run and having crossed the line as victors now pray that we also may win. If our church congregations are small let us bring to mind the tens of thousands of saints and angels with whom we sing and let us use their lives and teachings as guides to avoid heresy and confusion. But finally let our hearts be filled with hope when we meditate on what the Holy Spirit has done in them and what the Holy Trinity not only calls us to be but makes possible through obedience and trust.

Before moving on to our next topic let us pause for a moment and think about our patron saints and the business of naming our children (and in the case of converts choosing a new name when being received). All Orthodox people should have a patron saint and should try to draw close to them through prayer. We should try to remember that our patron saint has a special bond with us and the more we turn to them the deeper that relationship in prayer will become. Whole nations adopt particular saints for their protection and we as individuals should do likewise. We should be aware, however, that there are different customs within Orthodoxy concerning patron saints: for example in Serbia a particular saint is taken as the patron for the whole family and individual members do not choose different saints. There are also different customs with regard to names, some of which we shall explore but there are many more varieties of customs not included here.

When naming our children there are a number of ways that a saint may be chosen and all are acceptable. Some people feel a special connection with a saint and believe that the saint has prompted them to give the child into their care. Other people let the calendar guide them and choose the saint who is remembered on the date of the child's birth, or on the date of the baptism. It is the custom to consider our name day as more important than our birthday and if it is the custom within a family to exchange gifts on birthdays doing so on a child's nameday will help them to appreciate its importance and also to remember when it is.

There is also the issue of the name itself. If someone is converting to Orthodoxy and already has a name that is a saint's name then there is no need for them to take a new name. Some people will use their second name if their first name does not belong to a saint as I did when I was received as my second name is Stephen. If someone has a female form of a male saint's name, such as Stephanie, this is also a good Orthodox name to keep and there is no need to change it.

In many Roman Catholic countries it is not unusual to encounter people called Jesus but in Orthodox tradition this name is considered too holy to be used. Similarly Orthodox do not take the name Mary in honour of the Theotokos for the same reason but it is common to meet Marys or

Marias named after other saints called Mary such as Saint Mary of Egypt.

We change our names so that we are linked to a saint but there is a long tradition of people having their name changed to reflect a greater change in them. For example in the Old Testament Abram became Abraham and Christ changed the Apostle Simon's name to Peter. The effect of taking a new name can be quite dramatic and some people speak of how it has helped them to understand their new identity as members of the Orthodox Church. Each time we receive Holy Communion we are addressed by our new name and it can bring us into an awareness of ourselves as creatures made new in the waters of baptism.

We are told in Revelation that at the end of time Christ will reveal to us our true name that will be eternal. Names are more than a label which is why in so many ancient cultures soldiers captured in battle would never give their true name as they believed it revealed something important and profound about them. Christ instructs us to pray *in His name* which means to pray in His identity and will (and not just attach the phrase *in Christ's name* to the end of our prayers). When we take the name of a saint we should seek to emulate their holiness in all that we do, try to live up to the example they have set before us and do nothing to dishonour the precious name we have taken. Naming our children after saints also proclaims to the world our faith and our belonging to the Church on earth and in

Heaven, it declares our desire to live as inheritors of the holy traditions that have guided the generations before us.

The Angels

"Regiments of angels are distributed over nations and cities; and some are assigned to particular individuals."
~ Saint Clement of Alexandria

Many people outside the Church reject the belief in angels but in reality are rejecting the sentimental images presented to them through contemporary films and novels. In fact if this is the only perspective someone has of angels they are right to reject it because such nonsense has nothing to do with the awe-inspiring reality of who and what the holy angels are. Here we will consider what Tradition tells us about the angels: their nature and hierarchy, their different roles in God's service and finally what we Orthodox believe about Guardian Angels.

Although we use the word *angels* as a collective term it also refers to a particular group of angels within their hierarchy. From the Book of Daniel we know that there are a *thousand times ten thousand* of them in number, in other words countless ranks and these are ordered by God with specific names and roles. Orthodox belief is that there are nine ranks of angels and each of these is composed of three further hierarchies which are themselves each divided further into three ranks. This understanding is found as early as the Apostles: Saint Dionysius who was one of the original seventy records this belief which was commonly held. It is confirmed by many of the Church Fathers including Saint Ignatius, Saint Gregory the Theologian, Saint John Chrysostom and others. As we shall see the Church's faith was influenced by Jewish belief based on the revelations described in the Old Testament where we first read of the nine ranks.

At the top of the hierarchy are those angels which are permitted to be closest to God, the *Seraphim.* The word means *fire* or *flaming* and signifies their presence before the *flaming fire* of God as described in Hebrews (ch12 v2). Next are the *Cherubim* which translates as *great understanding* and reflects their role in giving understanding of God's wisdom both to man and to the other angels. Traditionally they are associated with the mysteries of God and their nearness to Him has transformed them into beings radiant with divine enlightenment. The third level are called *Thrones* which reflects how God mysteriously establishes His justice upon them and how they then carry God's justice to the affairs of men.

The next rank of three begins with the *Dominions* who express God's authority over governments, nations, and even our individual power over temptation. Next are the *Virtues* who are the angels God sends to support those who are struggling with the difficulties of life. They are also the means by which God permits his saints to perform miracles as they are understood to bring God's miraculous grace. The final rank in this group are the *Powers* who serve God in limiting the work of the demons but also in helping us to resist evil.

The third grouping has at its top the *Principalities*. Orthodoxy understands these angels to be the servants who maintain the order of the entire universe. The *Principalities* act to support good men in human society but also instruct the lower angels in God's will. Next are the *Archangels* who pronounce God's news and who are the means by which the prophets were given wisdom and knowledge. Finally are the *Angels* who of all the angelic hierarchy have most contact with humanity. Their role is to pray for us and guide us and there have been many examples of them acting to protect faithful Christians from danger.

In the Book of Genesis we read how God created the *heavens and the earth*. Christian tradition has always been that the angels were brought into existence before the physical universe and this is confirmed in Job where God reveals that *When the stars were made, all my angels praised me with a loud voice* (Job 38 v7). The angels were created along with *the heavens* which reminds us that *the heavens* is not a reference to the empty vacuum of space but the invisible world of spirits. The angels are incorporeal beings who have been made immortal by God's grace (they do not have immortality by nature). Since they do not have physical bodies they have no material needs or impulses and as Christ teaches us, do not marry or have the need to reproduce. Their nature also means they are able to travel anywhere instantly as they are not bound by physical laws. Angels have intelligence, will and personality like us but exceed us in their wisdom and understanding. This does not mean that angels are pure spirit however, since only God is this, but they have a form which is so fine it cannot be perceived with physical eyes unless God wills that they show themselves to us. Before man sinned he was equal to the angels in his power over the created order but through sin has broken his relationship with the universe: the regeneration of this relationship occurs as his growth in the image and likeness of God re-clothes him with Christ's glory.

Despite the specific activities of the different ranks of angels described above, we can summarise the work of the angels in simple terms as glorifying God in Heaven and fulfilling His will on earth. Since the angels worshipped Christ in Heaven we know that they will have continued to do so during the incarnation and it is astonishing to think of the countless ranks of angels which constantly surrounded Him during His earthly life. We are given glimpses of this: they supported Him after His fasting in the wilderness and as He prayed in Gethsemane, and at His birth the shepherds witnessed the sky filled with the heavenly host. Many of the Church's icons depict Christ surrounded by angels and when we look at them we should engage with their reality around Him but also with us. Of course it will be at Christ's second coming that we see the angels with Him and at that moment Christ tells us that they will be the reapers of God's harvest for which we should now be preparing ourselves. During this time of life the angels continue to help us prepare and though they do on occasion intervene and protect people physically, they more often guard and support us spiritually.

To fully understand how the angels interact with us we must recognise the nature of our own mind and thoughts. The Fathers describe us as having different levels or realms of thought and within these the mind is very distinct from the imagination. Within the soul the inner thoughts of the mind cannot be known by angels: this part of us is known only by God. But the imagination is an outer aspect of the soul and the Fathers teach that both angels and demons not only know what our imagination is filled with, but that they can prompt images and memories to dwell there. While the angels work to enable our imagination to be filled with moral goodness and holy events, the demons prompt base and selfish images which have the capacity to lead us to sin. This is why we must never trust our imagination when praying as the demons can easily fool us into imagining we are experiencing a deep relationship with God when in fact we may be full of sin and far from him. There are some approaches to prayer used by Roman

Catholics which deliberately use the imagination to create certain feelings or experiences: these are to be avoided by anyone wishing to remain safe. But the angels are so much more alert and aware than ourselves and so it is possible for them to perceive what we are likely to be thinking by the changes in our moods or by what we allow to dwell in the imagination. Even trained stage performers can use outward signs in someone's demeanour to guess at what they are thinking and so we should guard ourselves against any demon pretending to know our thoughts. Just as has been described earlier, the saints do not hear our prayers directly and so when we pray to the angels we do not need to do so aloud as God reveals our prayers to them. Again, as with the saints, it is important to remember that the angels do not want to be worshipped but desire that all praise be directed towards God.

Perhaps even more than angels, in general modern fiction has sentimentalised the idea of Guardian Angels to the point where many outside the Church consider them no more real than fairies or wishes made when blowing out the candles on birthday cakes. In fact the Church teaches us that at our baptism God appoints an angel to guide and support us and to pray alongside us. In His mercy God recognises our weakness and in His desire for us to be saved, gives us this great spiritual help. Like the saints our Guardian Angel does not mediate between us and God but in love for us longs for us to repent and live a worthy life. If we attempt to do this our Guardian Angel will remain with us but if we fill our lives with evil we can drive our friend away. As Saint Basil the Great writes:

The angel will not retreat from us, unless we drive him away by our evil deeds. As smoke drives bees away, and stench the doves, even so our stinking sin drives away from us the angel who protects our life.

The belief in Guardian Angels comes from both Jewish tradition and the New Testament. Michael the Archangel was believed to be the protector of the Hebrews and in the Book of Psalms we read *He will give His angels charge over you, to keep you in all your ways* (Psalm 91 v11). This tradition was certainly accepted by Christ Who referred to the angels watching over them when He warned about the consequences of anyone doing something that might prevent a child from entering the Kingdom of Heaven.

Our Guardian Angel cannot make up for our own lack of effort, commitment or love but will help us when we turn to God. Saint John of the Ladder recounts how his own spiritual growth was each day supported by his Guardian Angel and he encourages us to be sensitive to the work of our appointed helper: *If you feel sweetness or compunction at some word of your prayer, dwell on it, for then your Guardian Angel is praying with you* (The Ladder of Divine Ascent). Elsewhere in the same work Saint John assures us that when we face our trials with courage our Guardian Angel will grow nearer to us as we align our will with God's will.

As I waited for the ferry to carry me to Mount Athos I chatted with a man who served me coffee. Knowing where I was going he told me that the monks there live like the angels. He was referring to more than the outward aspects of their lives, and to even more than the countless hours they spent in prayer. All of us live more like the angels when we imitate their obedience to God. When we submit our will to God's will we make small steps into the Kingdom of Heaven. With the angels alongside us we need never fear that our spiritual path is ever a solitary one, and when we quietly pray alone we are assured that we are not alone. In our next chapter we will consider Orthodox belief in those angels who have rebelled against God but for now let us rejoice with those who reflect God's glory and let us never forget the mercy God has shown us in giving us such help.

From the Canon to our Guardian Angel:

O Angel of God, my holy guardian, keep my life in the fear of Christ, strengthen my mind in the true way and wound my soul with heavenly love, so that guided by Thee, I may obtain the great mercy of Christ God. Amen

Prayer To Your Guardian Angel:

O Holy Angel, who stands by my wretched soul and my passionate life: do not abandon me, a sinner, neither depart from me because of my lack of self-control. Amen

Who Is the Devil?

"Stubborn unbelief in the existence of evil spirits is in itself actual demonic possession, for it bids defiance of Divine revelation; he who denies the evil spirits is a person already swallowed by the devil."
~ Saint John of Kronstadt

Orthodox Christians understand that they live in a battleground and the whole of the New Testament witnesses to the fact that Christ came to earth to destroy the works of the devil. The quotation above from Saint John of Kronstadt would be difficult to read for many Protestant and liberal thinkers who have reduced the devil to an impersonal force or perhaps have explained away the existence of evil with psychology and other rational ideas. In the lives of some of the great ascetics we read of demons manifesting themselves in horrible forms and making direct attacks on Christian strugglers. Few of us are so advanced in the spiritual life that the demons need to be so obvious in their attacks on us but nevertheless all of us who seek to follow Christ have entered a spiritual warfare; it is vital that we know as much as we can about our enemy and how he fights against us. It was once a common expression that the most cunning trick of the devil is to convince people that he does not exist. Today in the twenty-first century we have seen such a decay in the moral values of man that the devil no longer even needs to hide: for those alert to him he can be seen in many aspects of popular culture, business, politics and Satanists even proudly tell the world of their allegiance to him. When Romania wanted to become a member of the European Union its government was told that it would have to change its laws and attitudes to homosexuality and abortion (which of course its leaders were willing to do) and so another Orthodox nation found its values being trampled under foot for the sake of profit. In this chapter we will look at the origins of the devil and how Tradition has drawn on Holy Scripture to understand how evil entered our world. We will look closely at how the devil fights against us and the effect he can have on our lives and we will reflect on why God permits not only the devil to exist but evil itself. But first we will remind ourselves of what Christ taught us.

When Christ taught us to pray He told us to ask God to *deliver us from the evil one*. He did not say *deliver us from evil* but *the evil one*. Again in his second letter to the Thessalonians Saint Paul uses the same phrase when he says *The Lord is faithful, and he will strengthen and protect you from the evil one* (2 Thes. 3 v3). Christ refers to the evil one as the *prince of this world* (John 12 v31) and elsewhere in the Gospel of Saint John he is called *the father of lies* (John 8 v44) and in the book of Revelation he is called the *deceiver* (Rev.12 v9). This shows us that the devil's main instrument of warfare is deceit and lies. The devil wishes to confuse us, mislead us, the devil tries to plant disbelief and fear in our hearts because his motive is hatred of God. But since the devil has no power to do anything against God he attacks those created in God's image. The devil expresses his hatred of God by trying to separate us from Him, and by encouraging us to refuse God's Kingdom.

The word *devil* comes from the Greek *diabolos* which means *divider* or *separator*. He was originally named *Lucifer* which means *light-bearing* and this title leads us to his origins. The Book of Enoch develops some of the details we find in Genesis where we read of fallen angels having interaction with human beings: many of the New Testament writers reveal their awareness of Enoch and it is this tradition that we find as the basis for the cosmology of the New Testament. Lucifer was an archangel created with free will. God did not create him evil nor did God create evil, but in misusing his free will Lucifer opposed the will of God and rejected goodness: he wanted for himself the worship rightly only ever given to God. This took place before the creation of the visible world and the Book of Revelation tells us that a third of the angels joined him in his rebellion

(Rev.8 v10). This vast number of angels became the demons and just as the angels in Heaven are ordered so the demons have specific ranks (called legions) which are ruled over by Satan. Saint Theophan the Recluse tells us that there are so many demons in the world that it is a blessing that we cannot see them because the sight would be so terrible it would overwhelm us and drive us insane. Through their voluntary fall their nature lost its fine angelic form and they were filled with darkness and spite and though they can appear to us in any form, their reality is an ugliness beyond imagination. But we must emphasise that the devil is not evil by nature but by will just as we have the capacity to choose and become evil.

The Bible tells us that the demons inhabit the aerial realms; they exist in the air above us. There is a story in the Desert Fathers of a monk who would never look up at the sky for this very reason (though we need fear no bad effect from doing so). Saint Paul describes them living in the air and many theologians have explained that this was the reason for Christ's death being on a cross raised into the air: he overcame them in the very realm they inhabit, his victory was absolute. All Satanic powers continue to be subdued by the power of the cross and we must use it as a weapon in our fight against them.

The most important thing we need to know about the devil is how he works against us and how we can protect ourselves against his attacks. The first thing to note is that though we recognise that demonic possession of people and objects is a reality (we exorcise the waters for baptism as well as the person being baptised), the real weapon against us is to lead us from the truth into delusion. And the demons' greatest desire is to lead astray those who seek to follow Christ. If God permitted the demons to do as they will they would kill us all but in His mercy God limits their actions and so they only have power over us when we join our will to their's. The reality is the demons seek to destroy us by fooling us into destroying ourselves, most notably in stirring pride and hatred within us. But just like the angels who cannot know the depths of our soul so the demons attempt to tempt us through the imagination as described in our previous chapter. Through lies they attempt to disturb us, make us fearful and doubtful of God's love and forgiveness so that we will try to find security elsewhere. The idols of pagan man are filled with demons, as Moses says in Deuteronomy, the Hebrews who turned to idols *sacrificed to demons not to God* (Deut.32 v17). There is something quite subtle being declared here, it is not simply that the demons dwell within such idols, which they do, but that the very act of placing our trust and faith in anything but God is a demonic trick because it separates us from the One Who is truly the answer to all our needs. Let us always remember that Saint Peter describes the devil prowling around us *like* a roaring lion, and not that he actually is one. The devil wants to convince us he is more powerful than he is, that his power is equal to God's, that he could be ever victorious. And the devil pretends to be more than he is in his attempt to distract us from seeing God for what He truly is. Let us remember the story of Job and how this man suffered the pain and disease caused by Satan but that he always remained in the hands of God because he continued to stay focussed on God: the devil wants us to look away from Christ and look instead to our fears or our needs or our accomplishments.

But we must not give in to fear. First we are assured that *God is faithful and will not permit us to be tempted beyond our strength, but with every temptation will give us an escape so that we may endure* (1Cor. 10 v13). God sees our struggles with evil and will never abandon us, however weak we may know ourselves to be. But we must also hold on to the knowledge that God's victory over Satan has already been achieved: Satan himself knows this and we must allow this truth to fill our hearts with peace.

Perhaps we may ask ourselves how the demons can lead someone who wants to be faithful to Christ to become so confused that they turn away from Him. The demons are cunning and do not openly call us to their rebellion but instead lead us away in tiny steps. When we begin to be negligent over tiny, seemingly inconsequential matters, the door has been opened slightly and the intruder has an entrance. When we knowingly commit unimportant, "little" sins, we begin to turn our focus away from God. When we allow our imagination to dwell for a moment on all the good things we could achieve if we had more money, or admire the beauty of a neighbour's spouse, evil begins to establish itself within us. When we think about all the effort we have put into keeping the fasts or attending extra church services we may easily begin to imagine we have made ourselves worthy of God's reward or earned His blessing. Each rank of the demons has a speciality and they see our weaknesses: they know precisely the particular temptations which reach our weaknesses. And so Saint Paul instructs us to put on the armour of God, he knew only too well the nature of this battle. All that Orthodox Tradition gives us is there to guard and guide us, it is armour and munitions used by generations of saints before us in the same war we now fight and which have proved so successful in defeating our enemy.

There remains for some people the nagging question of why God would allow not only the devil to "get away" with all this but even allow the existence of evil and suffering. The first point to make is that the devil has got away with nothing. Not only is his power destroyed through all that Christ accomplished in the incarnation but the devil knows that on the Day of Judgement he will be cast into torment. But still we might ask why God would allow us to suffer the evil he is permitted to perform. A number of the Church Fathers express the same reasons but perhaps one of the clearest explanations is to be found in the writings of Saint Maximus the Confessor. All that God does is good and everything He does with regards to us is for our salvation. By seeing the evil worked by Satan Saint Maximus says that God enables us to recognise the true nature of evil and so actively reject it. By struggling against temptations and passions Saint Maximus says that we learn how to distinguish between the virtues and the passions and our desire for virtue then becomes irrevocable and certain. But all of us have within us a mixture of virtue and vice and through this we are vulnerable to further falls. By allowing the devil to war against us God enables us to see and remember our spiritual disease and need for healing and so avoid falling into a state of apathy. While we struggle we may be blessed to achieve some victory and all too often we fall into pride because of it. Saint Maximus says that God permits the demons to fight us so that we never forget that it is by God's grace that any virtue is found in us and that he is the source of all goodness.

We must remember that the devil's power exists only in so far as we misuse our freedom. We must use our will to develop good habits such as prayer, fasting, attending church and reading spiritually nourishing books. We must develop self-awareness so that we guard our mind from dangerous and harmful thoughts but above all we must repent. The greatest weapon we have against the devil is humble repentance before God. We must see that there can be no compromise with evil in our lives, there is no middle ground in this war: in everything we do we either serve God or Satan. The demons will try to convince us of many lies such as claiming that we are all born guilty (original sin) but this is not true. Though we inherit the consequences of sin we are not rejected by God from our birth as guilty, we are spiritually sick and in need of Christ's healing. The demons mix their lies with enough truth to confuse us and we must embrace the Traditions and faith of the Church to avoid being led astray. Nobody has ever achieved perfection by being forced and God leads us into His perfection by love, teaching us how to use our free will in order to live fully in the Kingdom of God. We see in the devil the consequences of giving our will entirely to evil but in the saints we recognise the opposite. We must preserve ourselves from the devil's seduction by constantly attuning our hearts and minds to the truth. We cannot give away responsibility for our inner state by blaming everything on our enemy, though Satan will provide us with the tools, it is we who choose to use them. We keep ourselves safe by being obedient servants to the One Who loves us.

Our Appearance

"Therefore I tell you, do not be anxious about your life, what you shall eat and what you shall drink, nor about the body, what you shall wear. Is not life more than food and the body more than clothing? ...Why are you anxious about clothing? Consider the lilies of the field, how they grow, they neither toil nor spin, yet I tell you, even Solomon in all his glory was not arrayed like one of these."
~Matthew Chapter 6 v25-29

One of the mistakes we can make is becoming preoccupied with externals. Since we cannot see the workings of a man's heart we may foolishly make judgements on his outer appearance. Of course it is not our place to make judgements about anyone's standing before God, but we must especially guard ourselves against making assumptions based on someone's appearance. It really is none of our business how someone else looks and we may easily fall into sin if we allow ourselves to start thinking like this.

But when it comes to our own appearance we should be aware of the impact our appearance can make on others, for example we should not dress in such a way that could lead others to fall into the trap we have just described. On one level it is a trivial matter and not something to be overly concerned with, but on another level it is very important that we be aware of the effect we are having on other people, especially in church. In this chapter we will consider our clothes, our hair and beards and also the matter of women wearing scarves.

We are not required to slavishly follow rules without understanding why they are important: anything we do in this way will have little impact on the state of our heart. The rules and traditions of the Church should be understood as helping us to achieve a more spiritually-centred existence. As Orthodox Christians our desire is to live on earth knowing that we are called to be citizens of Heaven. Our outward appearance should not be so worldly and reflective of our times that we lose our true sense of identity. Similarly Christians have traditionally avoided a merging of the appearance of men and women, since we believe that God created us as man and woman, distinct and unconfused. In western culture there has been a move towards a merging of appearance and gender identity which is at odds with Christian thinking.

As a simple guide we can say that Christian women have avoided shaving their heads and men have not worn their hair in an effeminate style. If a man has long hair he should tie it back while in church. In many traditionally Orthodox countries women do not wear trousers in church but equally they avoid ostentatious clothing or anything that is overtly sexual. Very flamboyant clothing is intended to draw attention to the wearer and this is the last thing we should be tying to do amongst people attempting to focus on God. Modern styles often attempt to emphasise body shapes with tight fits or through the cut of the material and this should be avoided for the same reason.

It is worth noting that excessive use of make-up is entirely inappropriate in church for two main reasons. The first is a practical one: when venerating icons lipstick left on the image is unsightly and destructive of the painting. Women should ask themselves whether they would feel comfortable smearing lipstick over the actual feet of Christ: and if not why would they be content to do so on His icon? But the second reason is something we don't often talk about in polite society and may be something some women are not aware of. The purpose of many forms of make-up is to simulate the effects of sexual arousal. When a woman becomes sexually aroused her cheeks may become flushed and this is the look created by rouge. In this condition a woman's lips may become engorged with blood which is what lipstick simulates. A woman in a state of sexual arousal may find her pupils enlarge which darkens the eyes; again an effect simulated by mascara. Is it any wonder that some men find a woman in make-up more attractive? But women must ask themselves how appropriate it is to be attending church (or indeed anywhere else) while giving off these unconscious signals. In his comments on the decisions of the Sixth Ecumenical Council Saint Nikodemos the Hagiorite reminds us that the threat of excommunication hangs over women who paint their faces just as it does over men who pluck the hair from their faces. He goes on to criticise anyone who would want to dishonour the natural appearance that God gave us with *wicked beautifications.* Saint Gregory too instructs women not to *apply shameful paint to forms of God's, so as to be wearing masks and not faces.*

The nature of Orthodox spirituality reminds us of our poverty before the all-gracious and generous God. Our appearance should reflect something of this reality. In the world many people feel their personal worth is supported by displays of wealth, whether through flashy cars, clothes or jewellery. This mindset is directly opposed to the Christian understanding of a person's worth. Since we understand our entire value is based in our being created in God's image and in His continuing love for us, displays of wealth of this kind are faithless and offensive. If we then attend church adorned in gold we only display our worldliness and foolishness. Saint John Chrysostom encourages us not to adorn ourselves with *flamboyant decoration but with sobriety and good works*.

As Christians we are called to renounce materialism and vanity and our clothes and hair are a means of obedience to this calling. But we must also avoid dressing in order to tell everyone how humble we are. Displays of false humility are even worse than trying to dress like a king. If we are dressing with the purpose of making other people think in a certain way about us or if we are overly concerned with how we will be perceived then we are play-acting in one form or another. Our spiritual life must never be a role we play to convince others of something, this path leads to destruction and is a great weapon of the demons. Everything we do must be to please God not man, we must work to dress the inner man not the outer.

In some parishes it is the custom for women to wear head scarves and many women may find themselves questioning whether they should wear one. In my own parish it is not the custom to do this and my own wife does not do so. I point this out to affirm the right for women to make their own choice in this matter so that what follows cannot be misinterpreted as an attempt at implying anything prescriptive.

The first thing we should note is that covering the head did not begin amongst Christians but was a Jewish practice: in Chapter 5 of the Book of Numbers reference is made to uncovering a woman's head for a ceremony demonstrating that covering was the norm. We also find reference to head covering in Genesis Chapter 24 and Daniel Chapter 13, and many traditional Jews continue the practice today. Since the first Christians were Jews and continued to worship in the Temple in

Jerusalem it is not surprising that this would be one of the practices they continued with.

Saint Paul identified covering the head as bestowing honour on a woman and in his first letter to the Corinthians in Chapter Eleven he states explicitly that during prayer men must remove any covering of their heads while women must ensure that their heads are covered. It is a point he repeats a number of times in his letter to the young church in Corinth and he goes on to explain that women must do so in prayer because of the angels. At first this may raise all kinds of questions for modern readers but it is a point confirmed many times by different Church Fathers. When we pray we are in the presence of the angels, and Saint Cyril tells us that *the angels find it extremely hard to bear if this law is disregarded* (in his commentary on 1 Corinthians). The reason for this attitude is found in the Book of Enoch where we discover that fallen angels were filled with lust for women and that the covering of the head is to prevent this.

One further perspective on this is found in the Church's iconography. Almost without exception women saints are portrayed wearing head coverings (Saint Mary of Egypt is shown bare headed because she lived alone in the desert). If we look to the saints for examples in all things then can there be one any higher to follow than the Mother of God? In all icons of her she is shown with her head covered which sets the most blessed example of all for women to follow.

Covering of the head has been seen as a sign of humility in Church tradition, a declaration that a woman is in church to pray and not to glorify herself. Certainly for young men a woman with her head covered is clearly declaring her devotion to God and attempting to act modestly which sets the tone for their relationships. Of course if it is not the custom for women to wear head coverings in a local church then to do so can have the opposite effect: a scarf may draw attention to the individual wearing it and could leave others feeling uncomfortable (perhaps a sense that they are being judged). As mentioned earlier, this kind of showiness can be both a cause and consequence of pride and must be avoided.

When it comes to beards we must be clear that there is a difference between what is expected of the laity and of the clergy. A quick glance at old photographs will quickly confirm that it has for a long time been the tradition for Orthodox clergy to have beards and long hair. In the U.S.A. Saint Tikhon is often quoted as instructing his clergy to abandon these customs and many Orthodox priests in North America are often indistinguishable from Roman clergy in terms of their appearance. However, Saint Tikhon was using *economia* in order that Orthodox immigrants might find it easier to fit into the emerging American society that was their new home and it seems clear that he was not wishing to abandon Orthodox tradition in these matters as a permanent standard. So let us briefly consider why clergy wear their hair and beards this way.

The starting point for our understanding is in the Old Testament where long beards were a sign of devotion to God. Saint Paul wore his hair long and the Apostle James who was the first Bishop of Jerusalem was known to never cut his hair. Christ Himself is always portrayed with long hair and a beard in icons.

But some groups select verses from the First Letter to Corinthians to indicate Saint Paul's prohibition of long hair for men. In fact there are two words for hair in Greek, the first refers to the physical substance that grows from the head, but in Saint Paul's case he uses the word referring to hair as an ornament or decoration. The prohibition is against colouring or styling of the hair which maintains his earlier position about flamboyance and vanity. In fact short hair was recognised in the first century as a pagan custom which was rejected by both Jews and Christians alike.

A further source for this tradition lies in the influence on the Church of the desert ascetics. Monasticism had an enormous influence on worship (see later chapter) but also on the customs that became the norm for parish clergy. The desert hermits did not cut their hair and beards and only where an anti-monastic bias became prevalent in the West was their influence rejected. Monastics reject styling of the hair as being an act of vanity but there is another reason. Since Christ had long hair and a beard the imitation of his outward appearance sits alongside the struggle to imitate His perfect example inwardly.

Through the centuries the Orthodox tradition about beards has been a source of criticism from those outside the Church. Pope Gregory VII demanded that all his clergy shave and in times of Barbarian invasion western groups have clung to the shaven appearance in order to distinguish themselves from the "uncivilised" hoardes and achieve the look of classical Rome. So where does this leave the laity today?

While clergy are forbidden by the Sixth Ecumenical Council to shave their beard or bleach their hair in order to appear young and attractive no such injunction applies to the laity. But the underlying reasons for this ruling for clergy may be something the laity should engage with. Clergy must not seek for the sake of vanity to appear like "a young bridegroom", or desire to have the "face of a woman", and Orthodox tradition has always recognised the beard as being the difference in respect of appearance between a man and a woman. For clergy there is the added effect of identifying them as priests wherever they travel and so encourage them to maintain behaviour befitting of their rank. It is a matter for the individual layman to decide for themselves, but it is a decision they should try to make, free of the claws of vanity or social expectation. Of course a man's work may require him to adopt a particular appearance and even clergy are permitted to cut their hair and keep their beard short in order to earn a living.

When we speak about tradition it is clear that we can be talking about the whole Church Tradition or local traditions in a parish. If the local tradition seems to contradict something we have heard or read we are wise to follow what is local rather than assume we know better than everyone else. But tradition is important, it is as we have seen, one of the crucial ways that the Church has safeguarded what God has revealed. In the context of clothing and hair we can say that there are no absolute rules which we must obey, we are granted freedom by God to find liberation in Christ. But if we deliberately reject or break the traditions of the Church then it is often a sign of some spiritual problem which we must address within ourselves. The world is full of encouragement to declare individuality and personal expression, but in reality these are often masks for enslavement to the passions and wilfulness. We are not to try and become some kind of Orthodox clone that determines who and what we are, but we are to use discretion when choosing how to dress. We must submit ourselves to the ethos of Christian life which does and must run in contrast to worldly ideas. Removing the roots of our worldly thinking can often be helped by adopting traditional modes of behaviour and dress which help us to understand these different paradigms.

Saint Nicodemus warns us that the traditions and customs of the Church are not mere trifles which we are free to cast aside in favour of personal opinion or impulse. We do not select the "important" aspects of Church life to follow and discard those we consider peripheral. And yet we are not weighed down with a rigid set of rules but are offered freedom from that which binds us. Once we fully understand that we are all free to dress in whatever way we choose there is nothing to rebel against and there is no grand political statement being made by refusing to follow tradition. In fact true freedom from ego and self-centredness is discovered in being obedient to Church tradition.

A final comment must be that we must approach these matters always judging ourselves and never considering the choices of others. We are responsible before God for the choices we have made and have no idea what is going on in the lives of others. If we find ourselves thinking uncharitable thoughts prompted by someone's appearance we should condemn ourselves immediately and ask for God's forgiveness.

Some Final Thoughts

We have considered both doctrine and practice and we see that Orthodoxy is concerned with both what we believe and what we do. As Orthodox Christians we are no longer free to challenge or deny the Christian faith and must recognise the responsibility we have accepted of humbling ourselves and trying to speak on moral and spiritual issues with the voice of the Church rather than our own opinions. This does not mean we will never have things over which we struggle or have questions we need answering and we should approach our priest or someone we trust at these times. We must not fear questions since all truth is God's truth and it is important for us to have an intellectual honesty and not suppress our uncertainties.

But as we have looked at the various topics considered in this book time and again we have come back to the belief that the universe was made good and is being changed through Christ's victory over death. We should see our sin as a disease to be cured and recognise the Church as our place of healing. Orthodoxy proclaims that our purpose in life is to be deified, as Saint Peter says to become *partakers of the divine nature* (2 Peter 2 v10). Our salvation is not a legal transaction; it is not a matter of the devil being paid off or that God's anger had to be satisfied: Christ died and was resurrected to overcome the power of the devil which is the cause of death. This is our Good News and why our lives need not be ruled by fear. Christ has won, and our task is to run the race so that we may taste His victory. Modern Protestant thinking has convinced countless people that by simply repeating a certain formula of words they are assured of salvation. It is true that God's mercy extends beyond any sin we have committed but our salvation comes not in a single moment of enthusiasm but through a process of change and restoration: what we call *theosis*. Roman Catholicism focuses on our moral status with too little attention given to our inner state. It would be an over-simplification to say that Roman Catholicism is concerned with the outer man while Orthodoxy focuses on the inner, but we could argue that these are certainly key features of the two approaches to spirituality. At the heart of this difference is that Orthodoxy sees salvation as being the process of man becoming like God rather than working to change our moral standing before a judge who will find us guilty or innocent. The fall of Adam and Eve resulted from Satan's false promise that they would become like God if they acquired the knowledge of good and evil. Their desire was to truly be like God, but their mistake was in believing that they could be changed through their own means instead of through obedience. God's rules are not arbitrary laws intended to remove our freedom but the guidance God gives to help us become like Him through grace (not by nature). We read that Christ was obedient, even obedient to death on a cross. This supreme act of humility and obedience destroyed death for all eternity for those who turn away from lawlessness and live as children of God. And the place that we find God's guidance is in the Church. The traditions of Orthodoxy have been revealed in the power of the Holy Spirit as gifts from God to enable us to be transformed. If we live in obedience to the Church's traditions we are living in obedience to God.

Christ was resurrected as both God and man and so all humanity was raised with Him since He shared our nature fully. All men will rise at the end of time, Christ's actions were for all, but it is up to us to respond to the free offer of salvation He makes to us. The devil has persuaded many to believe that God will reject people in His anger, but Orthodoxy assures us that God's love for every man is eternal. However, the way we live our lives now either makes us ready to accept God's love or else we darken our souls with the rejection of love. Our task is to be purified, repent of our sins and be filled with God's grace so that at the final resurrection we experience God's love with joy. We must not let heretical ideas about the need for God's anger towards us to be satisfied damage our understanding of Him and potentially prevent us from seeking Him as we should.

The twenty-first century announced itself with great social change and as its decades pass we see this change gaining speed. National governments are abandoning the age-old understanding of marriage, the person and the place of religious belief within national life. Unaccountable organisations more wealthy and powerful than most governments now control political groups and determine the ways laws and social attitudes will be guided. Television drains people of precious time and subtly promotes its social agenda through distorted news and vulgar soap operas (the head of a US TV network recently admitted that he believed he could manipulate people's attitudes more quickly through one of his sitcoms than any campaign group or even government could ever hope to achieve). Our state schools are openly hostile to traditional values and Christian belief and many people sense this increasing rate of change in western culture. We must guard ourselves and our children against what we see now and what is to come and we can only do this by being as faithful as we can to the teachings of the Orthodox Church. We must be thankful that God has revealed to us the fullness of His Church and hold tight as the storms of the world try to tear us from the true path. So often the angels are recorded in the Bible greeting people with the words *Do not be afraid.* May we let this message grow in our hearts with the assurance that we are in God's hands, we have heard His voice and we have run to our Shepherd. The world and the devil cannot part us from Him so long as we reject their clamour and we only do this by following the ancient path to Christ revealed in the Church.

Glossary

Apostasy – when a Christian deliberately chooses to believe false teaching, it literally means *turning away*. As a sin it has a devastating effect on the individual and while for that person it is very serious the right belief of the Church as a whole is far more important since without this no one could know Christ.

Ascension – forty days after the resurrection Christ ascended into Heaven from the Mount of Olives. Christ's ascension completes the union of humanity with God since Christ ascended in the flesh.

Asceticism – in his efforts to develop self-discipline and to crucify the flesh the Christian enters a life of prayer, fasting and self-denial. The word comes from the Greek for *athlete* reminding us of Saint Paul's image of the Christian as one who runs a race and must maintain his efforts until the finish line is crossed. It is a great mistake of some western Christians to imagine that since they have proclaimed a faith in Christ they are assured of salvation.

Blasphemy – words or actions which aim to offend or debase God, the saints or sacred actions or objects. Blasphemy against the Holy Spirit is cited by Christ as the one unforgivable sin since it denies the saving action of God and is a rejection of God's help.

Burial – the internment of the body as a sign of faith in the General Resurrection.

Canonisation – the official recognition by the Church of someone's righteousness and that they are believed to be in a blessed state before God.

Chrismation – when Christians are baptised into the Orthodox Church they receive the Holy Spirit through this sacrament which involves the anointing with oil. It is the sacramental continuation of the laying on of hands that we find in the New Testament.

Communion – refers to the union between man and God and is commonly associated with the state that a person enters through the Eucharist but the holiness of our way of life is also vital.

Confession – we use this in two ways: first describing the witness to our faith and secondly the sacrament where we tell our sins to God before our priest and receive absolution (forgiveness or release from them).

Corruption – the condition or state of humanity after the fall from Paradise. It represents our sinfulness and mortality and is the cause of suffering.

Cosmos - this can mean both the world and the universe. It is often used when referring to the effect of sin and of the resurrection, both of which changed the cosmos.

Council – from the Book of Acts onwards the Church has always made its decisions regarding doctrine and Church order through gatherings of bishops. To equate authority in the Church with a single bishop was unknown for the first thousand years of the Church's life and continues to be unknown in Orthodoxy.

Creation – we can use this term to refer to God's action of bringing the universe into existence or as a noun for the cosmos itself.

Deification – the purpose of the Christian life, growing into the likeness of God through His Grace, a process of healing and restoration.

Departed – simply refers to the dead.

Devil – see Satan.

Energy – the uncreated Grace that comes from God which unites us to Him. It is distinguished from the essence of God which remains hidden from us (in mystery).

Essence – the mysterious nature of God in Three Persons which is beyond the perception or understanding of humanity. Essence refers to God's nature which is unknowable and eternally mysterious. Eternal life will therefore be an unending experience of growing in the knowledge of God without ever knowing Him completely since he is limitless.

Eucharist – from the Greek word for *thanksgiving* it refers to the sacrament of Holy Communion when Christians physically eat and drink the flesh and blood of Christ and so receive God's presence and strength.

Flesh – in the New Testament *flesh* refers to the fallen nature of man and identifies those influences of the fallen world which inhibit spiritual growth and tempt us into sin.

Free Will – man's ability to make moral choices. This choosing extends to the acceptance or rejection of God and is an aspect of what it means to be created in His image.

Glory – the revealed splendour of God.

Gospel – a term which has its roots in the ancient world where the ascension to the throne of a new ruler would be announced. It can be translated as *Good News* and refers to Christ's call to repentance in readiness for the Kingdom of God.

Grace – the uncreated energy of God experienced by Christians mainly through the sacraments. It is a gift from God and cannot be earned but is not bestowed on those who reject God.

Hades – similar to the Hebrew idea of Sheol, it is the Greek word for the place where the dead dwelt before the resurrection of Christ.

Heart – the location of one's spiritual centre where the Grace of God works within us.

Heresy – teaching which is opposed or differs from the doctrines of the Church. It is one of the most harmful and serious of sins.

Holy – from the Greek word *agios* meaning not of this world. *Agios* is where we get words like geologist and geography, and the prefix simply means not.

Hope – the trust in and sense of certainty about God's goodness.

Hypostasis – the union of existence which is applied to the Three Persons of the Holy Trinity and to the human and divine natures of Christ.

Illumination – can be applied to the sacrament of baptism and to the enlightening of a person by the light of God (which occurs at baptism and chrismation).

Judgement – the revealing by God of the true nature of a person's actions in terms of sin or righteousness.

Kingdom of God – in the Old Testament this was associated with the rule of God rather than a place. A person enters the Kingdom of God when they are obedient to God's will. The Kingdom of God is often used in the writings of the Fathers as meaning our participation in the divine life of the Holy Trinity.

Liturgy – the worship of God in Church services. The Divine Liturgy is the service of the Eucharist.

Logos – Saint John calls Jesus Christ, the Second Divine person of the Holy Trinity the Logos. It is a term used in Greek philosophy before the New Testament was written and expresses the idea not just of *word* but of self-utterance and the deeper sense of self-outpouring.

Man – throughout the Bible the word man refers to human beings rather than those who are male. Of all the creatures God made, only man was granted to be in the image and likeness of God and so is recognised as the pinnacle of creation.

Martyr – comes from the Greek word for *witness* and is usually used to describe those who give their lives for their faith in Christ.

Messiah – the Hebrew concept of God's chosen one. While many Jews expected an earthly king who would create God's Kingdom on earth Christ revealed a greater and more profound vision of His role which made the Kingdom available to every human heart.

Mind – sometimes used interchangeably with heart, the mind refers to the faculty of reasoning or the inner person.

New Age – a world-wide organisation consisting of many different groups and bodies which works towards a single world religion that mixes elements from many faiths. The New Age movement promotes occult practices (such as Yoga) under the guise of openness and inclusiveness that is founded on ideas of universalism and the rejection of a single, revealed and objective truth.

New Man – the Christian who is transformed by the Holy Spirit and released from the slavery to sin. It is used to distinguish from the *old man* which is those who are not united to Christ or changed by the Holy Spirit.

Nous – this is often associated with the heart as it perceives God. It is that part of us created in the image of God but which has been seen more as the mind in post-fall man.

Panagia – this Greek word translates as *all holy* and is a common term for the Virgin Mary, the Theotokos.

Paradise – used in two ways: first the place where Adam walked with God and second the eternal state of being with God after death.

Pascha – the Hellenised form of the Jewish word Pesach or Phaska, meaning passage or Passover.

Propitiation – the offering of Himself that Christ made through His suffering and death that leads to the reconciliation of man and God. It results in the liberation of man from sin and death.

Rapture – the heretical belief that God will gather up His Church before the time of tribulations preceding the return of Christ at the end of time.

Redemption – through His resurrection Christ has delivered us from death and the claims of Satan over us.

Remission – the forgiveness of our sins and the forgiveness we show others of their sins committed against us.

Repentance – from the Greek word metanoia which means to turn away from sin or to change one's mind. Repentance is an essential action necessary on the part of man to enter Paradise.

Satan – the angel Lucifer who led rebellion in Heaven and was cast out by God. The Greek word for devil literally means *separator* referring to his desire to separate us from God's love. While retaining free will the devil has become so corrupted by evil that all repentance is impossible for him and at Judgement he will be cast into eternal punishment.

Second Coming – the return of Christ at the end of time as Judge of the living and the dead to establish a new earth and a new Heaven.

Soul – the invisible, spiritual existence of a man united to his body.

Spirit – non-material being which has different uses in the Bible: first the Holy Spirit is the Third person of the Holy Trinity; second the immaterial part of a man which was breathed into the body at creation and finally it is the term used to describe the nature of angels which do not have physical bodies.

Theotokos – a term which literally means God-bearer but is often translated as the Mother of God. The term was agreed at the Council of Ephesus in order to maintain that it was truly God that was conceived in her womb.

Transfiguration – on Mount Tabor the three disciples witnessed the transformation of Christ and beheld His glory. This event is known as the Transfiguration and the word is also applied to the transformation that we experience through the Grace of the Holy Spirit.

Trisagion Prayer – prayers of *Holy God, Holy Mighty, Holy Immortal have mercy on us* which are sung three times. It literally means *thrice holy* and indicates the Three Persons of the Holy Trinity.

Vice – a sinful act which becomes a habit.

Virtue – a good or righteous action which is developed into a characteristic or pattern of behaviour.

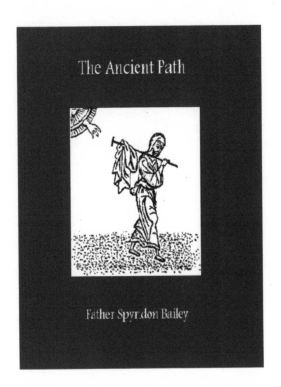

The Ancient Path

Father Spyridon Bailey

The Ancient Path is a collection of reflections based on quotations from the Fathers of the Orthodox Church. It is available from Amazon and Amazon Kindle.

JOURNEY TO MOUNT ATHOS

FATHER SPYRIDON BAILEY

Journey To Mount Athos describes Father Spyridon's encounters with monks and hermits during his pilgrimage to the Holy Mountain.

See Father Spyridon's author's page on Amazon for more books.

Lightning Source UK Ltd.
Milton Keynes UK
UKHW010626070122
396770UK00001B/173

9 781786 973924